GCSE Statistics
Foundation Workbook

This book is for anyone doing GCSE Statistics at Foundation Level.

This book contains lots of tricky questions designed
to make you sweat — because that's
the only way you'll get better.

It's also got some daft bits in to try and make the whole
experience at least vaguely entertaining for you.

What CGP is all about

Our sole aim here at CGP is to produce the highest quality
books — carefully written, immaculately presented and
dangerously close to being funny.

Then we work our socks off to get them
out to you — at the cheapest possible prices.

Contents

Section One — Data Collection

Planning an Investigation 1
Data Sources One 2
Data Sources Two 3
Types of Data 4
Classifying Data 5
Census Data and Sampling 6
Simple Random Sampling 8
Stratified Sampling 9
Biased Samples 10
Surveys — Questionnaires 11
Surveys — Interviews 13
Observing and Recording Data 14
Experiments 15
Simulation 18
Mixed Questions 19

Section Two — Tabulation and Representation

Frequency Tables 21
Summarising and Interpreting Data 23
Simplifying and Analysing Data 24
Bar Charts 26
Pie Charts and Dot Plots 28
Transforming Data 29
Frequency Graphs 31
Histograms & Frequency Distributions 33
Stem and Leaf Diagrams 34
Population Pyramids and Choropleth Maps 35
Scatter Diagrams 36
Time Series 37
More Diagrams, Problems and Errors 38
Mixed Questions 40

Section Three — Data Analysis

Mean, Median and Mode 42
Mean, Median and Mode — Discrete Data 43
Mean, Median and Mode — Grouped Data 44
Choosing the Best Average..46
Range, Quartiles and Percentiles 47
Interquartile Range 48
Box and Whisker Plots 49
Comparing Data Sets 50
Index Numbers and Crude Rates 51
Time Series 52
Time Series and Output Gap Charts 53
Correlation 54
Interpolation and Extrapolation...57
Estimation of Population 58
Mixed Questions 59

Section Four — Probability

Probability..61
Sample Space Diagrams 64
Venn Diagrams...65
Relative Frequency 66
Expected and Actual Frequencies 67
Probability Laws One 68
Probability Laws Two 70
Tree Diagrams 72
Conditional Probability..74
Mixed Questions 75

Published by Coordination Group Publications Ltd.

Editors:
Charlotte Burrows, Ben Fletcher, David Hickinson, Delene Kang and Alison Palin.

Contributors:
Andrew Ballard, Sally Gill and Janet West.

Proofreading:
Rosie Hanson and Andy Park.

ISBN: 978 1 84762 384 3

Groovy website: www.cgpbooks.co.uk
Printed by Elanders Ltd, Newcastle upon Tyne.
Jolly bits of clipart from CorelDRAW®

Based on the classic CGP style created by Richard Parsons.

Psst... photocopying this Workbook isn't allowed, even if you've got a CLA licence. Luckily, it's dead cheap, easy and quick to order more copies from CGP — just call us on 0870 750 1242. Phew!

Text, design, layout and original illustrations © Coordination Group Publications Ltd. 2010
All rights reserved.

SECTION ONE — DATA COLLECTION

Planning an Investigation

Flash, bang, whizzzzzz... Wooo. Welcome to the GCSE Stats workbook. The first topic to sink your teeth into is planning an investigation. You need to be able to think of a hypothesis for your investigation — this will explain clearly what you think is going to happen.

Q1 A head teacher wants to investigate how the weather affects how well the students in her school do in exams.
Write down **one** question that she could ask.

....

Q2 The Fixit drug company have discovered a new drug which they call "Poxfix". They think that Poxfix could be a cure for chickenpox.
What hypothesis should the Fixit drug company test to see if Poxfix works?

....

Q3 A sports scientist thinks that the more TV students watch, the more likely they are to be overweight and do badly in exams.
State **two** hypotheses that the scientist should test to see if he is right.

1. ....

2. ....

Q4 Last year, in the middle of summer, the Freezee ice cream company ran a leafleting campaign to promote their products. They wanted to test the hypothesis:
The campaign increased sales of ice creams per day.

	Average number of ice creams sold per day
Before leafleting campaign	486
After leafleting campaign	687

a) Does the data in the table support Freezee's hypothesis? ....

b) Give a reason for your answer.

....

SECTION ONE — DATA COLLECTION

Data Sources One

The first thing you need to decide is whether it's best to get your data from a primary or secondary source. Then you need to decide what type of biscuit to dunk in your tea. Hmmmmm... decisions, decisions.

Q1 Say whether each of these data collection methods gives **primary** or **secondary** data.

a) Using data from the 1901 census. ....

b) Doing an experiment to see how long students take to complete a puzzle. ....

c) Using temperature charts from a national newspaper. ....

Q2 In 2005 the Wonderme cosmetics company claimed that its anti-wrinkle cream was more effective than any other on the market. In 2009 a beauty salon used the Wonderme statistics when deciding which anti-wrinkle cream to promote.

a) Is the data used by the beauty salon **primary** or **secondary** data? ....

b) Give **two** disadvantages of using these statistics.

1. ....

2. ....

Remember — you collect primary data; someone else collects secondary data.

Q3 Complete the table by saying whether the data is **primary** or **secondary**.

Data	Primary or Secondary
You use data from the 2001 census on the number of rooms in people's houses.	
You use results from your research on sizes of spider webs.	
You use a pie chart from a magazine showing preferred beauty products.	

Q4 A market research company collects data on the amount spent on clothes per week by all the people living on Rosamund Street. The table below shows the ages of the people interviewed.

Age	Under 18	18-30	31-45	46-60	Over 60
Frequency	2	13	12	20	53

Cuthbert finds the company's data when he is doing research for a project on how school children spend their pocket money.

a) Is the data that Cuthbert uses primary or secondary data? ....

b) Give **one** reason why Cuthbert should not use this data.

....

Remember, your sources have to be relevant, accurate and unbiased.

SECTION ONE — DATA COLLECTION

Data Sources Two

Now you need to figure out how you're going to collect the data. Here's some questions on exactly that — how nice...

Q1 The makers of Raz washing powder want to test the hypothesis:

Clothes cleaned with Raz washing powder are whiter than clothes cleaned with any other brand.

How could the makers of Raz test this hypothesis?

....

....

Q2 Students at a school are doing a project on recycling in their local area. They decide to test the hypothesis:

Recycling levels rose after the council set up a collection service.

a) Do you think they should use primary or secondary data to test the hypothesis?

....

b) Describe **one** way in which the students could test the hypothesis.

....

....

Q3 The local council wants to investigate whether or not road traffic accidents at a certain junction are more likely to occur during the morning rush hour (between 8 a.m. and 9 a.m.) than any other time of day.

a) What data does the local council need to collect?

....

b) Should the local council use primary or secondary data?

....

c) Suggest a method that the local council could use.

....

....

....

SECTION ONE — DATA COLLECTION

Types of Data

Data can be qualitative or quantitative. Quantitative data can be discrete or continuous. Make sure you know the differences.

Q1 A music shop sells CDs, DVDs, tapes and some vinyl records.

State **one** example of qualitative data that could be collected by the shop.

....

Q2 Zac collects some data about his school. The data items are listed below.
Say whether each data item is qualitative or quantitative.

a) The colours of pants worn by the teachers. ....

b) The number of students late to school from each form on the first day of term. ....

c) The distance travelled to school by each student. ....

d) The star sign of each student. ....

Q3 Amy collects some data at her school sports day.
The data items are listed below.
Say whether each data item is discrete or continuous.

a) The number of competitors in each event. ....

b) The finishing times of each competitor in the 100-metre sprint. ....

c) The total number of points scored by each form at the end of the day. ....

d) The distances jumped by each competitor in the long jump. ....

Q4 a) What is bivariate data?

....

b) Say whether the bivariate data described below is discrete or continuous.

i) Shoe size and marks out of 20 scored in a science test.

....

ii) Heights and tail lengths of lesser spotted ferrets.

....

Section One — Data Collection

Classifying Data

Loads and loads of data can be pretty hard to analyse, so it helps to group it together to make it more manageable. All I can say is that it leads to one classy page...

Q1 The table shows the number of coins in the pockets of a random sample of 100 people.

Number of coins	0 - 5	6 - 10	11 - 15	16 - 30
Frequency	44	26	19	11

a) What are the lower class boundaries?

....

b) What are the class intervals in the table?

....

Q2 Fred asked each of his 30 classmates how long (to the **nearest minute**) it took them to eat their dinner. Here are the results he recorded:

42	13	3	31	15	20	19	1	59	14
8	25	16	27	4	55	32	31	31	10
32	17	16	19	29	42	43	30	29	18

Complete the table below.

Length of time (mins)	1 – 10	11 – 20	21 – 30	31 – 40	41 – 50	51-60
Tallies						
Number of people						

Q3 a) Write down a definition of a categorical scale of measurement.

....

b) The owner of a fast food restaurant collects data on the types of burgers sold in a week. The data is recorded in the table below.

Type of burger	Frequency
1	276
2	314
3	181
4	189

Key
1 – Hamburger
2 – Cheeseburger
3 – Chicken burger
4 – Vegetarian burger

i) What type of scale of measurement is the owner using? ....

ii) In the table, hamburgers are labelled 1 and cheeseburgers are labelled 2.

Does this mean cheeseburgers are twice as good as hamburgers? ....

SECTION ONE — DATA COLLECTION

Census Data and Sampling

Make sure you know what your population is — you can't do anything without knowing that.

Q1 Say what the population is for a survey looking into:

   a) The health effects of smoking on 20- to 30-year-old women.

   ....

   b) The number of trees in public parks in London.

   ....

   c) The average number of hours British squirrels spend juggling nuts.

   ....

   d) The pay of football players in the Premier League.

   ....

Q2 Use the appropriate word below to complete these sentences:

   sample frame   sample   census   sausage

   A sample frame can also be called a sampling frame.

   a) A .... is when you collect data about every member of a population.

   b) A .... is some members of a population.

   c) A .... is a list of all the members in a population.

Q3 Give **one advantage** of using **sampling** instead of a census.

   ....

Q4 An environmental group is investigating the water quality in all the lakes and council-owned ponds in Nottingham.

   You can't just choose any old population and sample frame — they have to be the best choice for your survey.

   a) What population should the environmental group use?

   ....

   b) What should they use as a sample frame?

   ....

SECTION ONE — DATA COLLECTION

Census Data and Sampling

Q5 a) Give **one advantage** of using **census** data instead of sample data.

....

b) 100 names are chosen at random from a telephone book for a sample of an area's population. Give **one** reason why this might produce a biased sample.

....

....

Q6 Dennis is carrying out a survey into the diet of the people who live in his town. He stands outside his local Plucky Fried Chicken fast-food restaurant and interviews the first 500 people to pass him.

a) What type of sampling has Dennis used?

....

b) State **one problem** of using this type of sampling.

....

Q7 Professor Xavier Entric is doing a research project on the lifespan of moorland dung beetles in the UK.

a) What population would Professor Entric use for his research?

....

b) Give one reason why Professor Entric would not use a census.

....

Q8 John and Kelly are collecting data about the distance their teachers travel to school in the morning. They each survey a random sample of 30 teachers chosen from the same sample frame — a list of all the teachers in their school.

John and Kelly get different results from their survey.

Explain why their results are not identical.

....

....

....

SECTION ONE — DATA COLLECTION

Simple Random Sampling

Ducks, jam, scissors and sausage dogs are all simple random things. But they have nothing to do with simple random sampling, which is selecting things at random from a sample frame.

Q1 Random numbers can be generated using random-number tables.
Give **two** other ways of generating random numbers.

1. ....

2. ....

Remember: choosing something at random means everything has an equal chance of being picked

Q2 Describe, in three steps, how to choose a simple random sample of 500 people from a list of 4000 names.

1. ....

2. ....

3. ....

Q3 Here's a list of places in the UK.

1. Lancaster	6. Bristol	11. Canterbury	16. Bradford
2. Birmingham	7. Glasgow	12. Cardiff	17. Bath
3. York	8. London	13. Blackpool	18. Auntie Bettie's house
4. Truro	9. Leeds	14. Norwich	19. Edinburgh
5. Manchester	10. Plymouth	15. Southampton	20. Armagh

Choose a simple random sample of 5 places using the random two-digit number list below.

12 26 04 11 01 26 04 29 09 18 13 30 07 22 18

Write your answers in this table:

Number	Place

Don't forget: you need to ignore any numbers that are repeated or are outside your range.

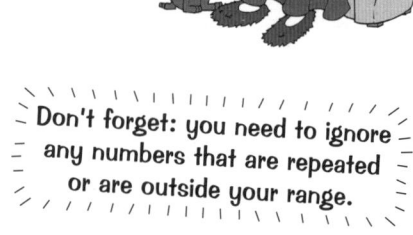

SECTION ONE — DATA COLLECTION

Stratified Sampling

Some tumbling rocks said "I can't get no satisfaction". But on this page there's stratisfaction, which is almost as good.

Q1 The table on the right shows how many staff work in a chain of restaurants. The manager wants to survey 10 employees using a stratified sample.

Waiting Staff	Bar Staff	Chefs	Total
50	30	20	100

How many waiting staff should be in the sample?

....

Q2 The Instyle chain of hair salons employs 1000 people across the UK.
They employ 100 receptionists, 50 salon managers, 250 colour technicians and 600 stylists.
They decide to use a stratified sample of 100 to find out about employee satisfaction.

How many of each type of employee should be in the sample?

a) Receptionists: ....

b) Salon Managers: ....

c) Colour Technicians: ....

d) Stylists: ....

Q3 Fred is doing a statistical project on the distances travelled by students to his school.
The table below gives a breakdown of the numbers of students in each year group at Fred's school.

Year Group	7	8	9	10	11	Total
Number of Students	400	403	401	197	199	1600

Don't forget that the proportion of any group in a sample has to be the same as the proportion in the population.

Fred decides to take a stratified random sample with 40 students.

a) Give **one advantage** of using a stratified sample.

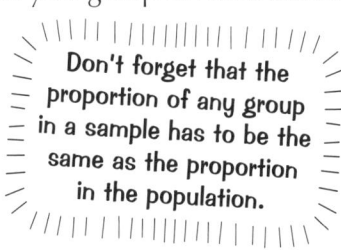

....

b) How many Year 7 students would be in the sample?

....

c) How many Year 10 students would be in the sample?

....

SECTION ONE — DATA COLLECTION

Biased Samples

I spy with my little eye something beginning with b... If you think the answer is bias, well done, give yourself 10 points — spotting bias is what this page is all about.

Q1 Millom University Chemistry Department wants to find out the influence of its marketing on sixth-form chemistry students in the UK.

They compile a survey and send it to all the students at the nearest sixth-form college.

a) Give **two** reasons why this sample is biased.

1. ....

2. ....

b) What population should the Millom University Chemistry Department be sampling from?

....

Q2 Fred is trying to find out why people do or don't use public transport.
He surveys a sample of 100 people passing through the town bus station between 5.30 p.m. and 6.30 p.m. on a Monday evening.

a) Give one reason why Fred's sample is biased.

....

b) Say how Fred could improve his sample to avoid bias.

....

....

We would like to apologise for the lack of graphic to accompany this question. We were hoping a bus might turn up.

Q3 The local council in Yeovil wants to find out whether their residents prefer to shop at out-of-town shopping centres or on Yeovil High Street.

They interview a sample of 1000 people.

The interviews were conducted on Yeovil High Street on Saturday morning.

a) Write down a reason why this sample is biased.

....

b) What population should the council have sampled from?

....

Section One — Data Collection

Surveys — Questionnaires

Questionnaires are a great way to gather information. But you need to think carefully about how you design, distribute and collect them so you get the information you want.

Q1 A pilot study is when you test your questionnaire on a small group before sending it out to the sample. Why is it useful to carry out a pilot study?

....

....

Q2 a) Give **one** advantage of using online questionnaires over paper questionnaires.

....

b) Give **one** disadvantage of using online questionnaires.

....

Q3 Brugton University wanted to find out what its ex-students are doing now.
It has a list of the ex-students' home addresses for the time when they were at the university.
It decided to send a questionnaire to the ex-students in the post.

a) Give **one** advantage and **one** disadvantage of distributing the questionnaire to its ex-students by **post**.

Advantage: ....

Disadvantage: ....

It asked the ex-students to send the completed questionnaire back in the post, but only 28% of the questionnaires sent out were returned.

b) Suggest **two** ways that they could improve the response rate.

1. ....

2. ....

Q4 Emma runs a one-day 'Lion Taming for Beginners' course at the local sports centre.
She hands out a feedback questionnaire at the end of the lesson and asks the students to hand the questionnaires back into the sports centre reception.

a) Give **one disadvantage** of distributing the questionnaire by this method.

....

b) Give **one disadvantage** of collecting the questionnaire by this method.

....

Typical... well at least they were only one page late.

SECTION ONE — DATA COLLECTION

Surveys — Questionnaires

Q5 Stanley is researching the use of the school canteen.
He asks this question to a sample of students at the school:

How often do you use the canteen? Tick one of the boxes.

Very often ☐   Quite often ☐

Not very often ☐   Never ☐

Remember — questions should be easy to understand, non-leading, unbiased and unambiguous.

a) Give one criticism of Stanley's question.

....

b) In the space below, write a better question that Stanley could use to find out how often students at his school use the canteen.

Q6 Neeta is writing a questionnaire to find out about how students travel to her school.

a) Write one **open** question that Neeta could use.

....

b) Write one **closed** question that Neeta could use.

....

....

Q7 The Milkychoc chocolate company uses the following question to find out about the public's taste in chocolate:

Do you agree that Milkychoc chocolate is the tastiest around?

a) Give **one** problem with this question.

....

b) How would you improve the question?

....

....

SECTION ONE — DATA COLLECTION

Surveys — Interviews

Interviews aren't just for celebs to promote their new book. You can use them to gather data too — so make sure you know their advantages and disadvantages.

Q1 Say whether each of the questions listed below is more suited for use in a face-to-face **interview** or in a **questionnaire**.

a) *Tick the boxes which describe what you had for breakfast today. You can tick more than one box.*

☐ Toast ☐ Cereal ☐ Boiled Egg
☐ Tea or Coffee ☐ Fruit Juice ☐ Other

....

b) *Why did you buy a house in this area?* ....

c) *Did you travel to work by bus this morning?* ....

d) *Have you knowingly broken the law in the last twelve months?* ....

Q2 a) Give **two** advantages of using an interview instead of a questionnaire.

1. ....

2. ....

b) Give **two** disadvantages of using an interview instead of a questionnaire.

1. ....

2. ....

Q3 The government is carrying out a survey. They consider two methods of collecting data from a widespread sample of households:

Method A: Devise a questionnaire and use it in a face-to-face interview.

Method B: Devise a questionnaire and use it in a phone survey.

Give one advantage of using method B instead of method A.

....

....

Observing and Recording Data

Data can be obtained by counting or measuring and then recorded in a data sheet or, if you have a swish-widget-doo-hickey, you can use data logging to do both.

Q1 Karen wants to know the average weight of a banana.
Circle the appropriate degree of accuracy for her measurements.

   kilograms   centimetres   tonnes   grams

Q2 The following data is being collected by pupils at the Albus Academy:

- Pupils' favourite drink at lunchtime.
- Pupils' heights.
- Time taken to travel to school by each pupil.
- Number of people living in each pupil's household.

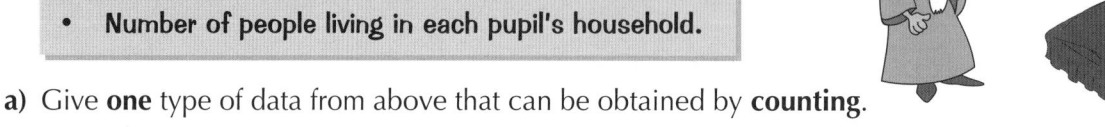

This data sheet spell needs more work — they keep coming out as bed sheets.

   a) Give **one** type of data from above that can be obtained by **counting**.

   ....

   b) Design a data capture sheet in the space below to record the number of people living in each pupil's house.

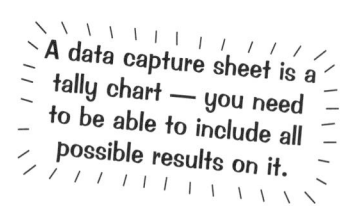

   A data capture sheet is a tally chart — you need to be able to include all possible results on it.

Q3 Abbie and John are measuring fabric to make a tea towel. John suggests they measure the fabric to the nearest m and Abbie suggests the nearest cm.

   a) Whose units should they choose? Explain your answer.

   ....

   ....

   Abbie measures the fabric to be 30 cm wide and 40 cm long to the nearest cm.

   b) What are the smallest and largest possible values for the actual width and length of the tea towel?

   Smallest: .... wide   .... long

   Largest: .... wide   .... long

Section One — Data Collection

Experiments

There are lots of things to keep in mind when you're designing or doing an experiment — what variables you need to change and measure, what you need to keep constant, what type of experiment to use, have you got clean underwear on, that sort of thing...

Q1 A group of people were asked to name their favourite hot drink. The results are shown in the table.

	Under 25	25 and over
Tea	5	12
Coffee	14	12
Hot Chocolate	4	3

What are the **two** variables used in the table?

1. ....

2. ....

Q2 Number these types of experiment 1 to 3 in order of how much control the scientist has over any extraneous variables (1 = most control, 3 = least control).

a) .... Laboratory Experiments   b) .... Natural Experiments   c) .... Field Experiments

Q3 A biologist measures the effect of air humidity on rates of plant growth.

a) What is the **explanatory** variable?

....

b) What is the **response** variable?

....

The explanatory variable is the thing you change, the response variable is the thing you measure.

Q4 Say whether each of the experiments below is a laboratory experiment, a field experiment or a natural experiment.

a) A wellie manufacturer measures average rainfall each month to see whether this has an effect on sales of wellies.

....

b) A teacher heats three identical beakers of water to 30 °C, 40 °C and 50 °C to see whether water temperature affects the amount of sugar needed to make a saturated solution.

....

c) A supermarket chain collects data on whether the location of soap powder in the store affects its sales.

....

SECTION ONE — DATA COLLECTION

Experiments

Q5 Tess the cook suspects that potatoes cook faster when they are cut up into smaller pieces.

Give an example of an **extraneous** variable in this experiment.

....

Q6 *"Listening to loud music makes people drive faster."*

Write down **two extraneous** variables for this hypothesis.

1. ....

2. ....

An extraneous variable is any variable that could affect an experiment but is not the explanatory or response variable.

Q7 A sensor automatically measures the temperature inside a nuclear reactor every 15 minutes.

a) Name the data collection method used.

....

b) Say why this is an appropriate data collection method to use.

....

Q8 Amy is weighing newborn kittens to make sure they are healthy and growing properly. She records the weight of each kitten to the **nearest gram** and puts the data in a table:

	Week 1	Week 2	Week 3	Week 4	Week 5
Patch	110	200.8	280	368	54
Tiger	102	194	275	372	443
Felix	112	203	281	837	451

Identify any rogue values in the data and give a reason for each of your choices.

a) Value: .... Reason: ....

b) Value: .... Reason: ....

c) Value: .... Reason: ....

SECTION ONE — DATA COLLECTION

Experiments

Q9 100 volunteers are to be used to test a possible cure for the common cold in the form of a tablet.
They have all been infected with the same cold virus for the experiment.
The scientists split the volunteers into **two groups**.

   a) How many of the 100 volunteers would you give tablets to for the experiment?

   ....

   b) What would you do with the remaining volunteers?

   ....

   c) State one variable which you would seek to keep constant throughout the experiment.

   ....

Q10 Cleo wants to investigate the hypothesis:

   "as her fitness improves her resting heart rate will decrease"

   She decides to do a 20-kilometre cycle ride every day for 20 days to improve her fitness.
   Before each trip she uses a heart-rate monitor to record her resting heart rate.

   a) Why is it important that she measures her heart rate at the same time before each trip?

   ....

   b) How could she improve the reliability of her results?

   ....

   ....

Q11 Two tennis coaches watched some matches and gave the players ratings out of 10 for their serves.

   a) Explain how inter-observer bias could affect the ratings.

   ....

   b) Describe how the coaches could reduce the effects of inter-observer bias.

   ....

   ....

SECTION ONE — DATA COLLECTION

Simulation

If you're doing the AQA course this page is especially for you. If you want to simulate some data you need random numbers. Down the back of the sofa would be a great place to check but it's a lot easier to look in a table.

Q1 a) A random-number table needs to be generated for a simulation. Each number is made by using the first three figures of a random number produced on a calculator *(using 'Ran#' on mine)*. The first two random numbers have been put in the table for you.

Complete the table below, using your calculator to generate the remaining random numbers.

Random-number tables are used to simulate random events happening.

639	225						

b) When spun, a fair coin has an equal chance of showing heads or tails. Design a method of using the completed random number table to simulate spinning a fair coin.

....

....

Q2 The 2-digit random-number table below is to be used to simulate rolling a fair dice.

43	41	32	20	31
76	77	25	93	34
24	65	54	13	31

Mel decides to use the first digit of each random number to represent the roll of dice. She ignores the random number altogether if the first digit is a seven or more.

a) What is the other digit that Mel should ignore? ....

b) Complete the table below for 10 simulated rolls of the dice using Mel's method.

Roll	1	2	3	4	5	6	7	8	9	10
Value	4									

c) Mel looks at the rolls in her table and sees that there are three 3s. She concludes that 3 is the most likely roll.

  i) Is this conclusion correct? ....

  ii) Explain your answer.

  ....

Phew, the end of the section. By now you should be a virtuoso of data collection techniques, so bring on the data analysis...

Mixed Questions

Just what you always wanted — some questions covering different bits of Section One so you get loads of practice. Oh goody.

Q1 The head librarian of a village library decides to hand out a questionnaire to find out what types of books the **local residents** prefer. She gives a questionnaire to everyone as they leave the library that week.

   a) Is the data collected primary or secondary data? ....

   b) Give **one reason** why the data might be biased.

   ....

   Included in the questionnaire is a closed question asking how many books people borrow from the library per week.

   c) i) What is a closed question?

   ....

   ii) Give **one advantage** of using closed questions in a questionnaire.

   ....

   Here is another of the questions in the questionnaire:

   | What is your favourite type of book? |
   | Reference ☐   Fantasy ☐   Crime ☐ |

   d) Give **one criticism** of this question.

   ....

Q2 A head teacher wants to find out the views of students at his school regarding school dinners. The head teacher decides to use a sample of 75 students, stratified by year.

   a) How many students from year 11 should be included in the sample?

Year 7	Year 8	Year 9	Year 10	Year 11	Total
176	179	190	197	200	942

   ....

   ....

   b) Give one advantage of gathering views from a sample of students, rather than using a census.

   ....

SECTION ONE — DATA COLLECTION

Mixed Questions

Q3 Hayley, the owner of a small factory, thinks that half an hour of exercise in the morning before work would improve her employees' performance.
She decides to test her hypothesis by asking her employees to exercise before they get to work. Then they fill in a questionnaire about their performance at the end of the day.

a) What would be the **response variable** in this experiment?

....

b) Give **one extraneous** variable that could affect this experiment.

....

c) Give **one problem** with Hayley's method.

....

....

Q4 The owner of a small cinema wants to investigate whether his customers would be interested in watching 3D films.

a) State the **population** for this investigation. ....

He hands out a questionnaire to each person and asks them to put the completed questionnaire in a box at the entrance to the cinema.

b) Give **one disadvantage** of the owner collecting the questionnaires in this way.

....

Only 23% of all the questionnaires handed out are handed back in.

c) Suggest one way that the owner could increase the number of responses.

....

The owner wants to simulate which film people who come to the cinema will see.
The cinema currently has four films showing, so he assigns them the numbers 1–4.

1 = Copper Man, 2 = Toys Tale, 3 = Next Destination, 4 = Robert Hoodie

d) Assuming that the probability of seeing each film is equal, use the random number table below to simulate which film the next 5 people will see.

Hint: Use the first digit from each number and read left to right starting at 186.

186	478	607	299	537	086
768	923	333	861	251	331

Write your answers in this table:

Digit					
Film					

SECTION ONE — DATA COLLECTION

Section Two — Tabulation and Representation

Frequency Tables

Frequency tables are a good place to pick up some REALLY EASY MARKS — so make sure you know this stuff like the back of your hand.

Q1 Zoe plays pool in her youth club. She writes down how many of her pool balls are left on the table at the end of every game.
Here are her results:

3, 0, 7, 2, 1, 3, 1, 6, 4, 0, 5, 2, 0, 7, 3, 2, 1, 1, 0, 0, 0.

a) Complete the frequency table below for Zoe's data.

Pool Balls	0	1	2	3	4	5	6	7
Tally								
Frequency								

b) How many games does Zoe record in total?

....

Q2 Fiona records how many birds she sees visiting her bird table each day.
Here are Fiona's results:

3, 8, 5, 7, 4, 3, 2, 6, 4, 7, 5, 4, 4, 6.

a) On how many days did Fiona record the number of birds?

....

b) What was the highest number of birds that Fiona saw visit her bird table in one day?

....

c) Complete the frequency table below for Fiona's data.

Number of birds	0	1	2	3	4	5	6	7	8	9
Tally										
Frequency										

d) What number of birds did Fiona see most often?

....

e) How many birds did Fiona count in total?
Hint: Make sure you multiply the frequencies by the number of birds before you add them all up.

....

Frequency Tables

Q3 Here are a list of marks which 32 pupils gained in a History test:

> 65, 78, 49, 72, 38, 59, 63, 44, 55, 50, 60, 73, 66, 54, 42, 72,
> 33, 52, 45, 63, 65, 51, 70, 68, 84, 61, 42, 58, 54, 64, 75, 63.

Complete the tally table making sure you put each mark in the correct group.
Then fill in the frequency column.

Marks	Tally	Frequency
31-40		
41-50		
51-60		
61-70		
71-80		
81-90		
	TOTAL	

Q4 A group of Year 10 pupils are given 'yellis' scores.
These help predict how well they will do in their GCSEs.
Their teacher lists them below:

> 5.1, 6.2, 7.9, 6.0, 4.1, 5.6, 7.0, 6.8, 6.7, 5.3, 6.3, 7.2, 5.0, 5.8, 3.1.

Complete this grouped frequency table:

Score (s)	Tally	Frequency
$3.0 < s \leq 3.5$		
$3.5 < s \leq 4.0$		
$4.0 < s \leq 4.5$		
$4.5 < s \leq 5.0$		
$5.0 < s \leq 5.5$		
$5.5 < s \leq 6.0$		
$6.0 < s \leq 6.5$		
$6.5 < s \leq 7.0$		
$s > 7.0$		

Remember, fill in the tallies first, then you can just write down the frequencies.

SECTION TWO — TABULATION AND REPRESENTATION

Summarising and Interpreting Data

For the exam, you might need to know how to summarise bivariate data and interpret tables of real-world data. So make sure you can do these questions.

Q1 A garden centre measures the height and width of 15 begonia plants. Here are the results:

| Height (cm) | 20 | 15 | 10 | 18 | 12 | 21 | 13 | 15 | 17 | 16 | 22 | 24 | 12 | 11 | 9 |
| Width (cm) | 21 | 14 | 9 | 16 | 14 | 19 | 15 | 13 | 20 | 15 | 19 | 20 | 13 | 15 | 14 |

Complete the two-way frequency table below to summarise this data.

Width (cm)	Height (cm) $h \leq 12$	$12 < h \leq 18$	$h > 18$
$w \leq 12$	1	0	0
$12 < w \leq 18$	4	5	0
$w > 18$	0	1	4

Q2 This two-way table shows the heights of fifty married couples.

Men	Women $h \leq 1.4$ m	$1.4 < h \leq 1.8$ m	$h > 1.8$ m
$h \leq 1.5$ m	5	2	1
$1.5 < h \leq 1.9$ m	4	17	3
$h > 1.9$ m	3	2	13

a) How many couples consist of husbands who are taller than 1.9 m and wives who are taller than 1.8 m?

.... 13 ....

b) How many wives are 1.4 metres tall or less?

.... 12 ....

Q3 One hundred vehicles on a road were recorded as part of a traffic study. Use this two-way table to answer the following questions.

	Van	Motor-bike	Car	Total
Travelling North	15			48
Travelling South	20		23	
Total		21		100

a) How many vans were recorded? 35

b) How many vehicles in the survey were travelling south? 52

c) How many motorbikes were travelling south? 9

d) How many cars were travelling north? 21

Section Two — Tabulation and Representation

Simplifying and Analysing Data

Top tip: When you've got loads of data, it's helpful to simplify it. This will make the data easier to interpret, although you'll lose some of the original detail.

Q1 Each member of a class of 32 throws the javelin. Their distances are rounded to the **nearest metre** and summarised in the bar chart below.

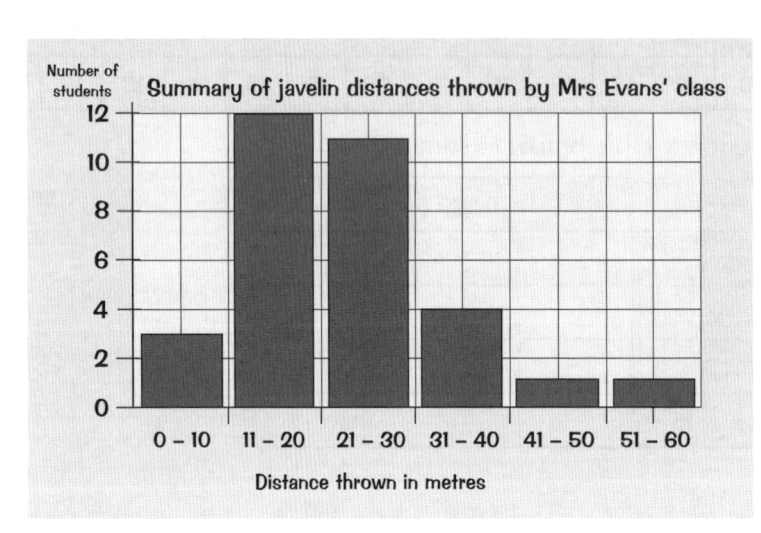

Summary of javelin distances thrown by Mrs Evans' class

(Bar chart: 0–10: 3, 11–20: 12, 21–30: 11, 31–40: 4, 41–50: 1, 51–60: 1)

There are several ways you can simplify data — totalling, converting to percentages or grouping.

a) Complete the following table, using data from the graph.

Distance (m):	0 – 10	11 – 20	21 – 30	31 – 40	41 – 50	51 – 60
Frequency	3					

b) Why might rounding to the nearest metre have distorted the data?

....

....

c) The table is simplified by using larger class widths for the distances. Complete this new table:

Distance (m)	0 – 20	21 – 40	41 – 60
Frequency			

d) i) What do you notice about the first and second groups in the new frequency table?

....

ii) What important detail has been lost by the simplification?

....

SECTION TWO — TABULATION AND REPRESENTATION

Simplifying and Analysing Data

Q2 A pet shop owner has kept a record of the number of each type of animal she sold over 4 years:

Animal	2006	2007	2008	2009
Rabbits	68	90	112	120
Rats	30	28	35	36
Guinea Pigs	45	42	30	40
Stick Insects	20	18	10	9
Parrots	4	6	16	12

a) Complete this new table for the total number of animals sold each year:

Year	2006	2007	2008	2009
Total				

b) What does this table show you about the total number of animals sold?

....

c) Now look back at the original table. What detail has been lost by totalling the data?

....

....

Q3 The table below shows how some schoolchildren travelled to school in Terms 1, 2 and 3.

	Term 1	Term 2	Term 3
Car	8	5	5
Walk	5	6	15
Bus	7	14	5

a) Complete the simplified version of the table below using percentages:
Hint: Use the total for each term to work out the percentage.

	Term 1	Term 2	Term 3
Car	40%		
Walk	25%		
Bus	35%		

b) Give **one** disadvantage of the simplified table. Explain your answer.

....

....

Section Two — Tabulation and Representation

Bar Charts

Bar charts are nice little fellas and, if you know your stuff, can earn you some easy marks. So have a go at these...

Q1 The pictogram below shows the number of books borrowed from a mobile library over five days.

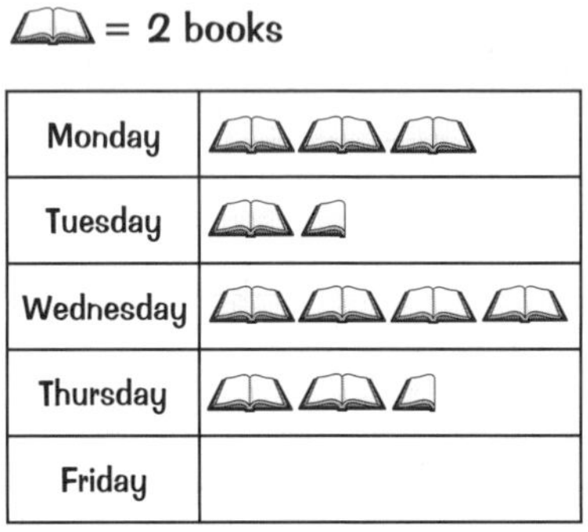

📖 = 2 books

Monday	📖 📖 📖
Tuesday	📖 📖
Wednesday	📖 📖 📖 📖
Thursday	📖 📖 📖
Friday	

a) How many books were borrowed on Tuesday?

....

b) How many more books were borrowed on Wednesday than Tuesday?

....

c) Seven books were borrowed on Friday. Complete the pictogram above.

Q2 Megan records how many people choose pizza or pasta in her Italian restaurant. The multiple bar chart below shows the results over one week.

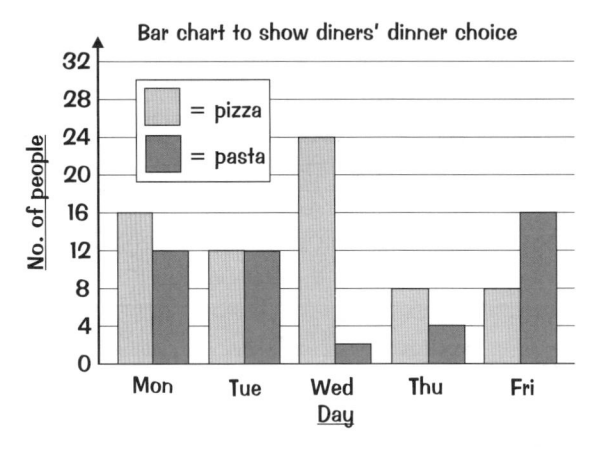

Bar chart to show diners' dinner choice
(□ = pizza, ■ = pasta)

Mon: pizza 16, pasta 12
Tue: pizza 12, pasta 12
Wed: pizza 24, pasta 2
Thu: pizza 8, pasta 4
Fri: pizza 8, pasta 16

a) On which days was pizza more popular with Megan's customers?

....

b) On which day did she have the most customers?

....

SECTION TWO — TABULATION AND REPRESENTATION

Bar Charts

Q3 The graphs below show statistics on marital status for people over 65 years old in Knottington.

Marital status of people aged 65 and over: by sex and age, 2008

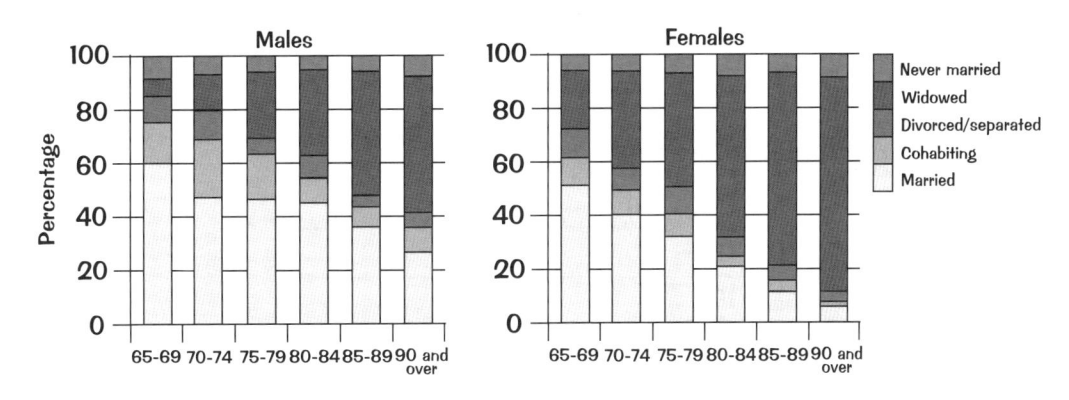

a) What proportion of males aged 65-69 are married? ....

b) What proportion of females aged 65-69 are married? ....

Q4 The chart below shows the number of each gender that smoke in 'Cigsville' by year.

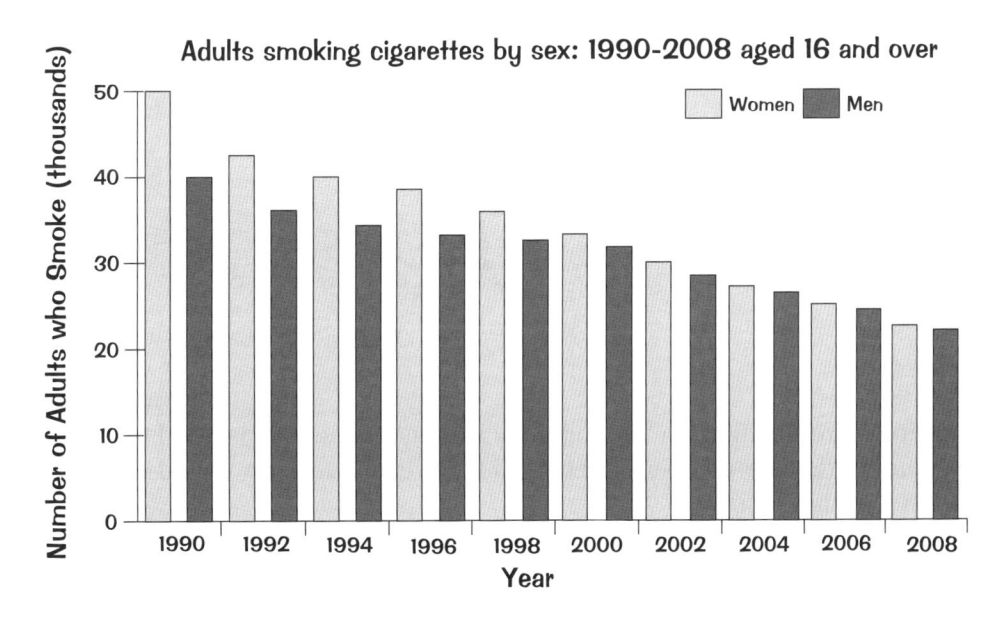

a) Describe the overall trend in smoking habits from 1990 to 2008.

....

b) What was the difference between the numbers of men and women smoking in 1990?

....

SECTION TWO — TABULATION AND REPRESENTATION

Pie Charts and Dot Plots

You'll need to remember that there are 360° in a circle to answer questions on this page. For those *AQA* folk there's also a cheeky little question on dot plots... lovely.

Q1 Pupils at a school were asked about their activities at weekends. The results are shown in the table. Complete the table and then draw the pie chart using an angle measurer.

ACTIVITY	HOURS	WORKING	ANGLE
Homework	6	6 ÷ 48 × 360 =	45°
Sport	2		
TV	10		
Computer games	2		
Sleeping	18		
Listening to music	2		
Paid work	8		
Total	48		

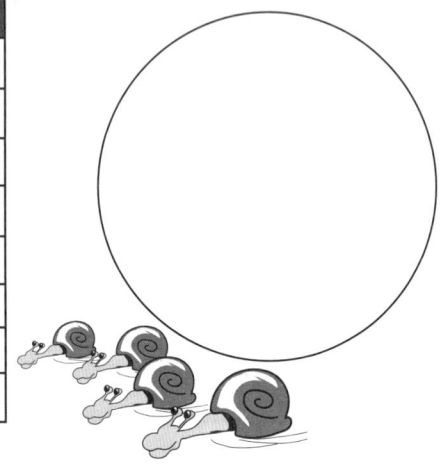

Q2 *(AQA only)* The table below shows the favourite colours of 14 nursery school children. Draw a dot plot to represent the data.

Colour	Number of children
Blue	6
Red	3
Green	4
Yellow	1

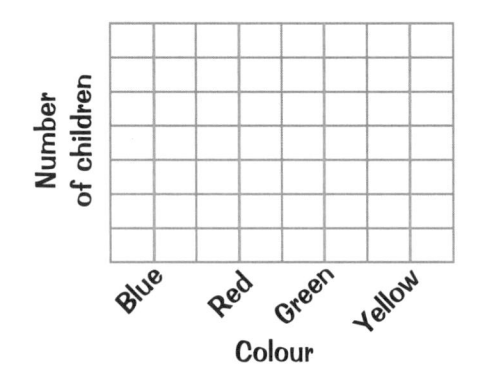

Q3 Sandra is giving a presentation on her company's budget. She has decided to present the budget as a pie chart. The company spends £54 000 each week on various items, which are shown on the pie chart below.

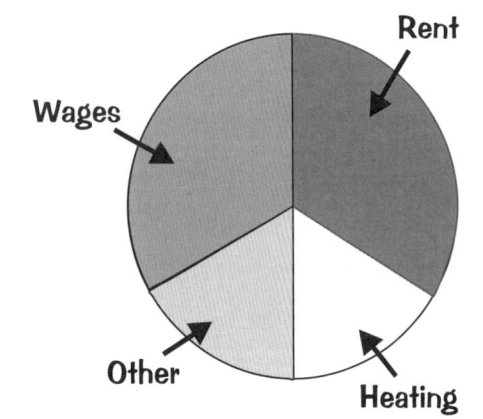

a) What fraction of the budget is spent on wages each week?

....

b) How much money is spent on wages each week?

....

SECTION TWO — TABULATION AND REPRESENTATION

Transforming Data

There is a tricky little pie chart on this page to get you thinking — make sure you brush up on angles in circles for that one...

Q1 This bar chart shows the number of sweets of different colours in a large packet.

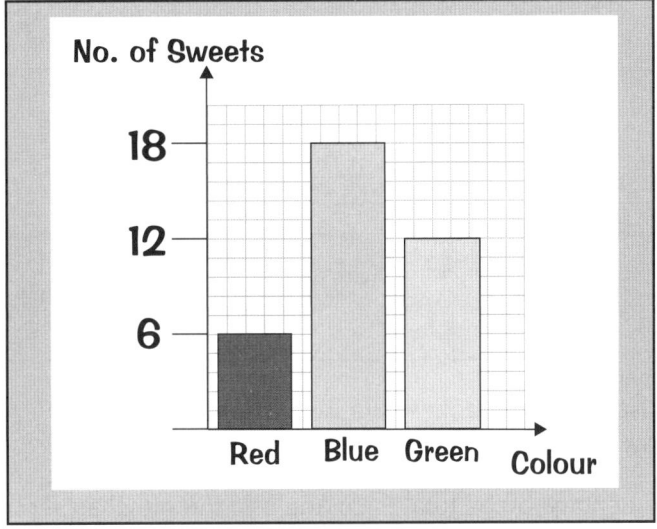

a) How many sweets in total are there in the packet?

....

b) Transform this data into a pie chart. Show all of your workings.

....

....

....

....

....

....

....

....

A TOP TIP — Once you've got the total number of sweets, you can calculate each angle using this formula:

$$\text{Angle} = \frac{\text{Number in category}}{\text{Total number}} \times 360°$$

SECTION TWO — TABULATION AND REPRESENTATION

Transforming Data

Q2 A newspaper asked **200** people what type of website they visited most often. The pie chart below shows the data they collected.

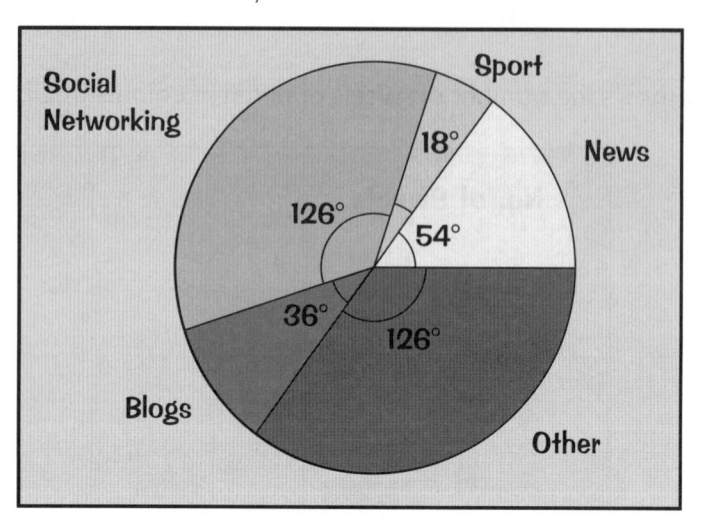

Pie chart showing: Social Networking 126°, Sport 18°, News 54°, Other 126°, Blogs 36°

Kirsty wants to use this newspaper's data in a school ICT project, but wants to show it as a bar graph.

Percentage = (angle ÷ 360°) × 100%

a) Work out the percentage of the total each angle in the pie chart represents. Show all of your workings.

....

....

....

b) Change the percentages into numbers and plot the data on the grid as a bar chart. Show all of your workings.

....

....

....

....

....

....

....

Remember to label the x-axis.

[Grid with y-axis labelled "Number of people" from 0 to 80]

Section Two — Tabulation and Representation

Frequency Graphs

If you've got discrete data, you can draw a vertical line graph. If your data is continuous, like height or speed, you can draw a frequency polygon or a cumulative frequency graph.

Q1 Megan counts the exact number of sweets in each of 15 packets.
Her results are shown in the frequency table below.
Draw a vertical line graph of the results on the grid below.

Sweets	14	15	16	17	18
Frequency	3	6	4	0	2

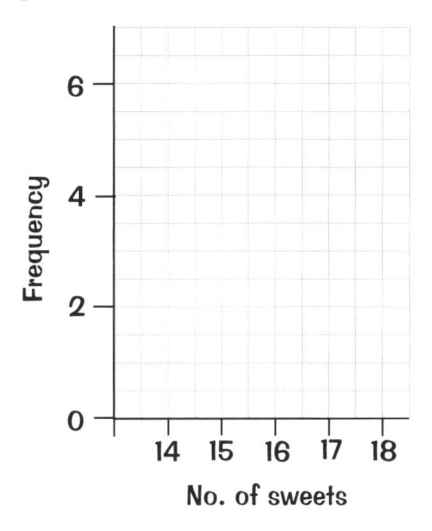

Q2 Donna works in a local butterfly house and records the wingspans of each of the butterflies in the table below.

Wingspan (cm)	$0 < w \leq 4$	$4 < w \leq 8$	$8 < w \leq 12$	$12 < w \leq 16$	$16 < w \leq 20$
Frequency	3	7	4	5	1

Draw a frequency polygon for Donna's data on the grid below.

Remember — for a frequency polygon you should plot the frequency against the midpoint of each class.

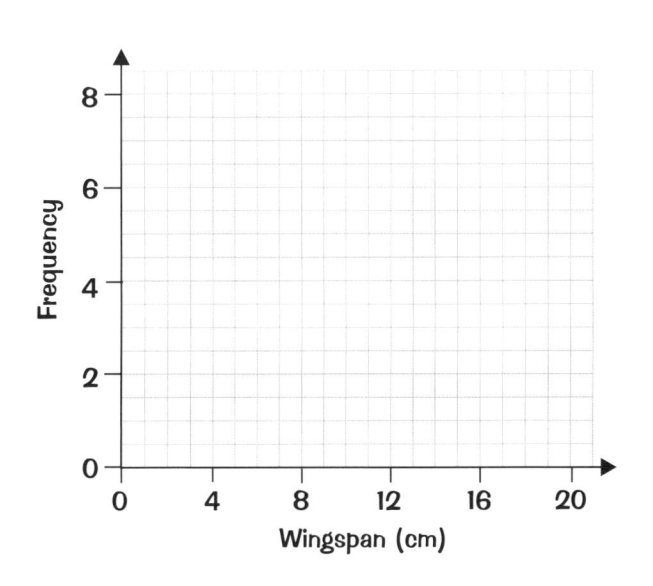

SECTION TWO — TABULATION AND REPRESENTATION

Frequency Graphs

Q3 Jo regularly goes out on a Friday night. Jo records her spending in the grouped frequency table below.

Jo's Spending

Spending (£)	Frequency	Cumulative Frequency
0 ≤ £ < 5	1	
5 ≤ £ < 10	4	
10 ≤ £ < 15	6	
15 ≤ £ < 20	2	
20 ≤ £ < 25	1	

a) Complete the cumulative frequency column in the table above.

b) On the grid below, draw a cumulative frequency polygon for Jo's data.

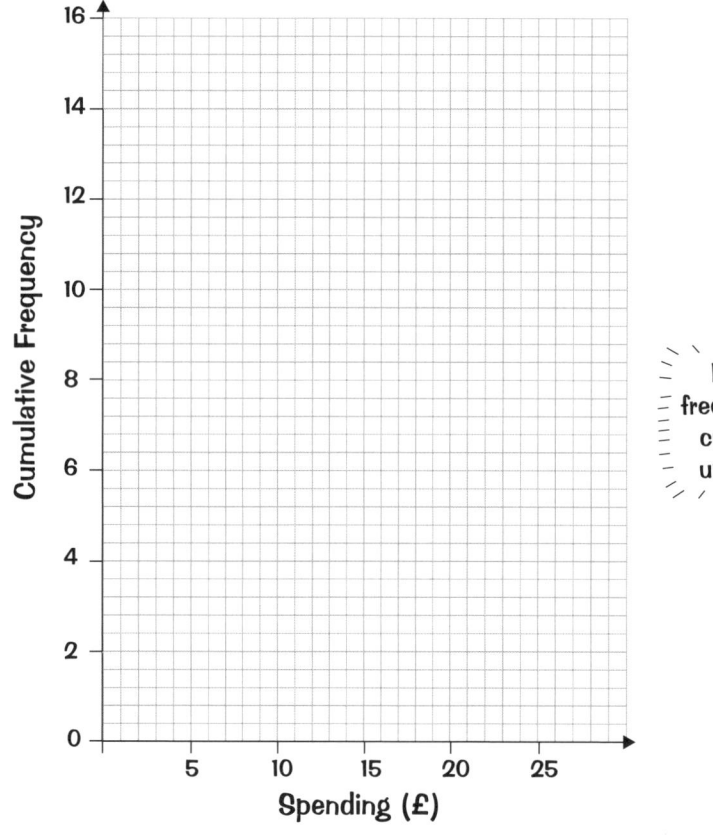

Remember — for a cumulative frequency graph you should plot the cumulative frequency against the upper boundary for each interval.

c) Use your graph to estimate the number of times she has spent £11 or less on a Friday night.

....

SECTION TWO — TABULATION AND REPRESENTATION

Histograms & Frequency Distributions

Histograms can be used to represent continuous data. They can also show you the shape of a frequency distribution. Have a bash at these questions...

Q1 The table below gives some information about how long it took 15 goats to fetch a frisbee.

Time, t (s)	Frequency
0 < t ≤ 20	3
20 < t ≤ 40	5
40 < t ≤ 60	2
60 < t ≤ 80	4
80 < t ≤ 100	1

Use the information in the table to draw a histogram on the grid on the right.

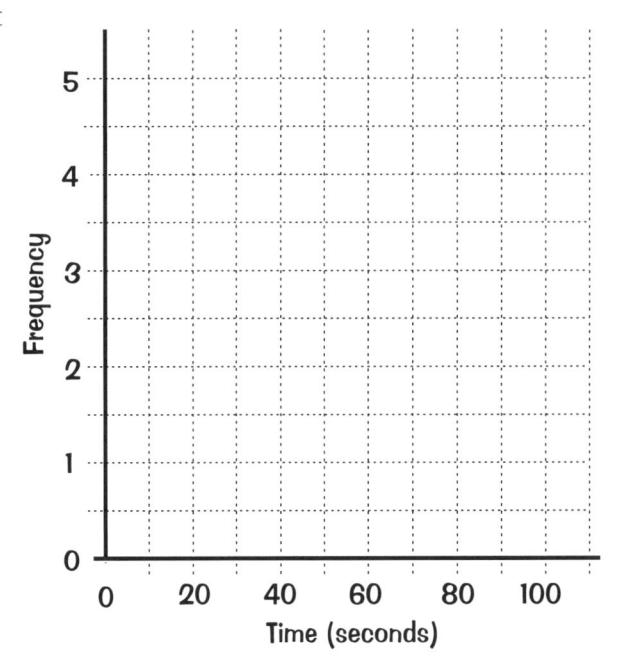

Q2 Two spinners are spun and the scores on each added together. This is done 30 times for three different pairs of spinners. The results are shown in the graphs below.

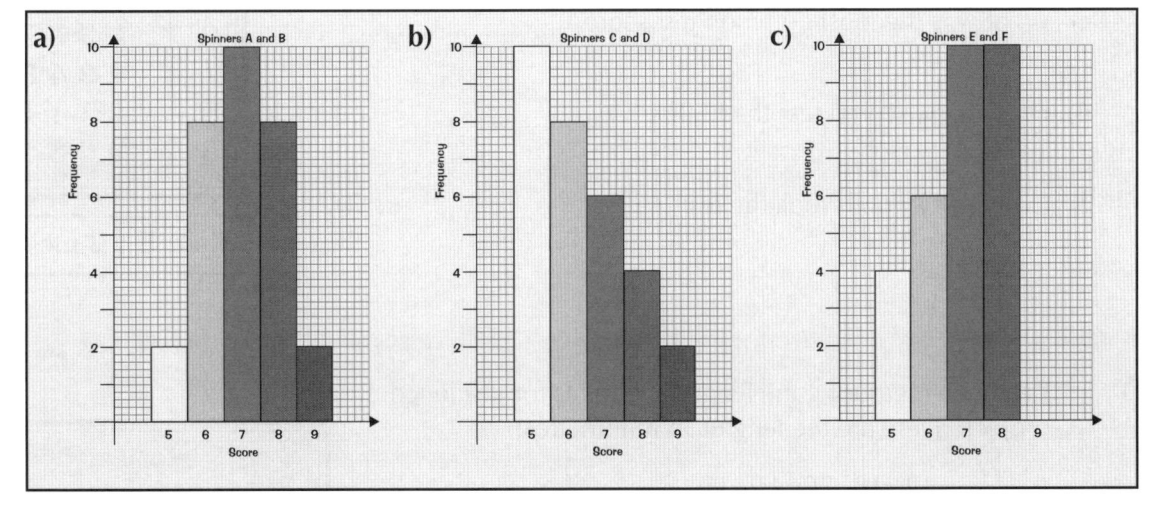

For each pair of spinners above, describe:

i) the **skew** of the distribution.   ii) the **range** of total scores.   iii) the **modal score(s)**.

a) i) ....

b) ii) ....

c) iii) ....

SECTION TWO — TABULATION AND REPRESENTATION

Stem and Leaf Diagrams

Stem and leaf diagrams... everyone loves a bit of nature in their lives... remember, these can be used to show the shapes of distributions and are useful for comparing sets of data.

Q1 This stem and leaf diagram shows the ages of people in a cinema.

1	2 2 4 8 8 9 9
2	0 1 1 2 5 6
3	0 0 0 5
4	2 5 9
5	
6	8

Key: 2 | 5 means 25

a) How many people in the cinema were in their twenties? ....

b) Write out the ages of all of the people in the cinema below.

....

....

Q2 This stem and leaf diagram shows the exam scores of a group of Year 9 pupils.

a) How many pupils got a score between 60 and 70? ....

b) How many scored 80 or more? ....

c) What was the most common test score? ....

d) How many scored less than 50? ....

e) How many pupils took the test? ....

3	2 3
4	6 8 8
5	1 2 2 3 6 6 9
6	1 5 5 5 8
7	2 3 4 5 8
8	0 1 1 5
9	0 2 3

Key: 5 | 2 means 52

Q3 I've been measuring the length of beetles for a science project. Here are the lengths in millimetres:

12 18 20 11 31
19 27 34 19 22

a) Fill in the stem and leaf diagram on the right to show the results above.
(Hint: Fill in the key first.)

b) From your stem and leaf diagram, find the range of the data.

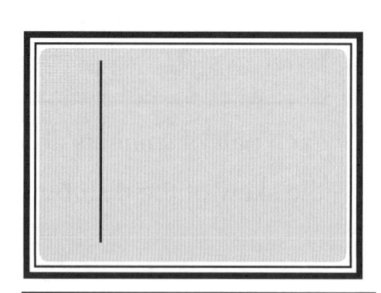

Key: |

....

SECTION TWO — TABULATION AND REPRESENTATION

Population Pyramids & Choropleth Maps

Population pyramids and choropleth maps aren't as bad as they seem... make sure you can <u>interpret</u> both of these for the exam... off you go.

Q1 These two population pyramids compare the distribution of ages in Broughtonia and Moorland:

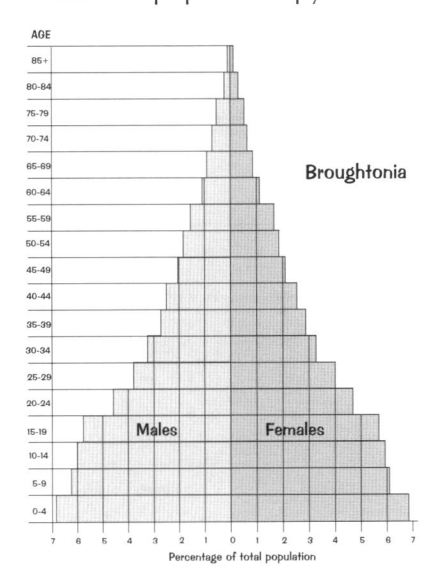

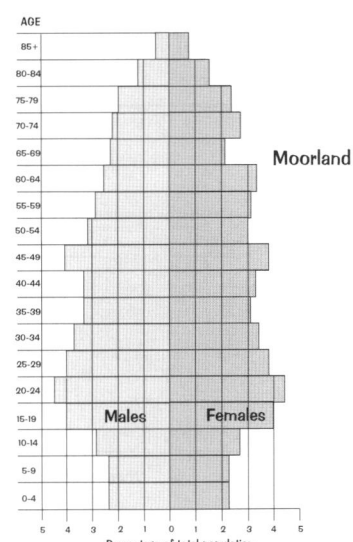

These population pyramids might look a bit scary, but don't worry — just think of them as two bar charts that have been put side by side so you can compare stuff.

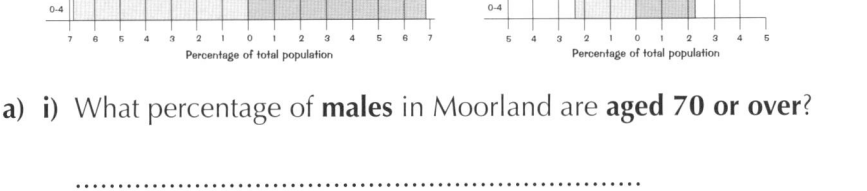

a) i) What percentage of **males** in Moorland are **aged 70 or over**?

....

ii) What is the **equivalent** percentage for **Broughtonia**?

....

b) What does Moorland's pyramid indicate about the birth rate in recent years?

....

Q2 The choropleth map on the right shows the population density of eight districts of a city.

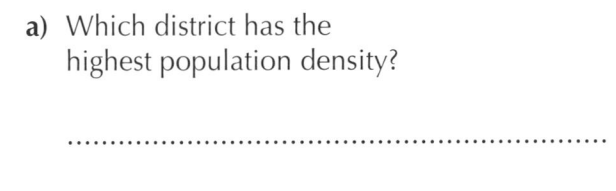

Key:
Population density (people/km^2)
- 0-99
- 100-199
- 200-299
- 300-399

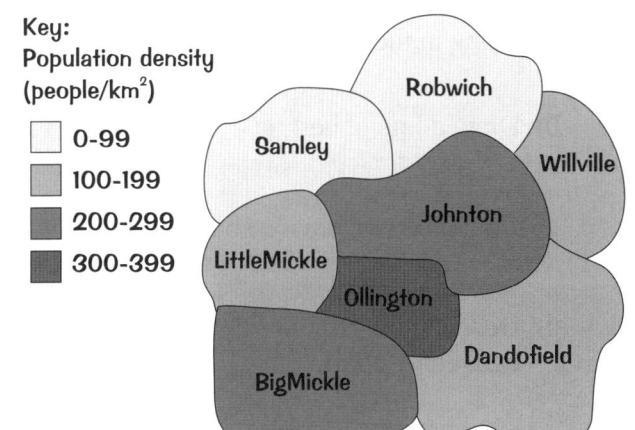

a) Which district has the highest population density?

....

b) What is the population density of Bigmickle?

....

c) Which regions have a population density between 0-99 people/km^2?

....

SECTION TWO — TABULATION AND REPRESENTATION

Scatter Diagrams

Look carefully at scatter graphs to see if there's a relationship between the variables — if there is, you can draw a 'line of best fit'.

Q1 What relationships (if any) would you expect to see between the pairs of variables given below? Where possible sketch the **lines of best fit** that show these relationships on the axes below.

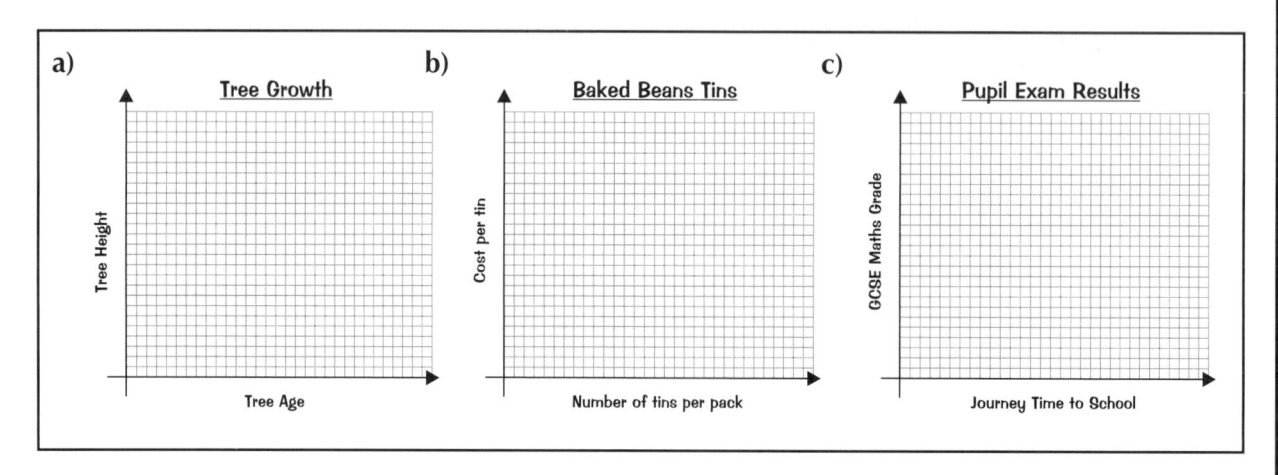

a) **Tree Growth** — Tree Height vs Tree Age

b) **Baked Beans Tins** — Cost per tin vs Number of tins per pack

c) **Pupil Exam Results** — GCSE Maths Grade vs Journey Time to School

Remember — Correlations between variables can be positive, negative or not exist at all.

Q2 The scatter graph shows the data from the table below. **Three** points have yet to be plotted.

x	3.5	3.0	6.0	4.0	5.5	2.0	1.0	5.5	4.5	5.5	7.0
y	4.0	5.0	3.0	0.0	3.0	7.0	6.5	3.5	4.0	4.0	2.0

a) Complete the graph on the right, filling in the missing points.

b) Draw a line of best fit.

c) Circle the **one** obvious outlier.

d) Describe the relationship between x and y.

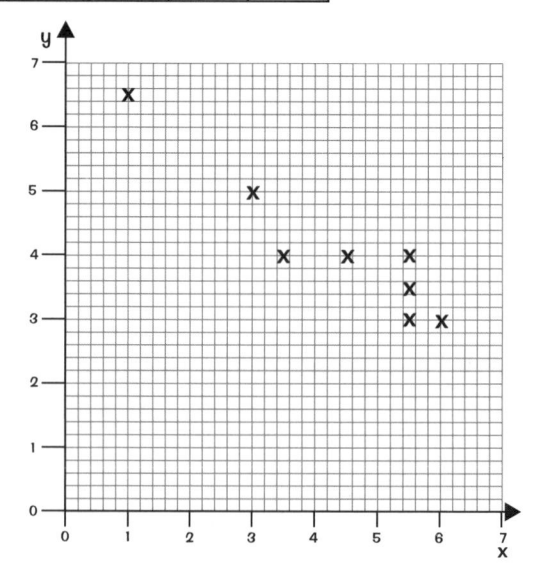

....

....

SECTION TWO — TABULATION AND REPRESENTATION

Time Series

Time series charts can be plotted if you have data which has been collected at regular time intervals. For example, sales figures, rainfall etc. You need to know how to <u>plot</u> them, draw a <u>trend line</u> and <u>interpret</u> them...

Q1 a) Time series charts sometimes show seasonal fluctuations. What are seasonal fluctuations?

....

Here are three time series charts:

i) ii) 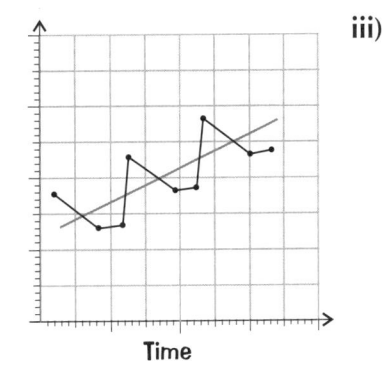 iii)

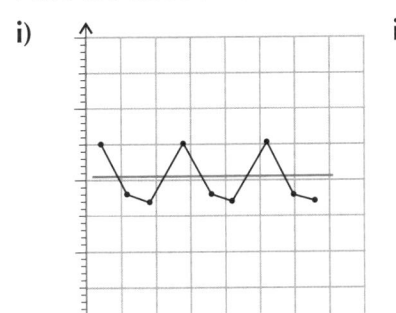

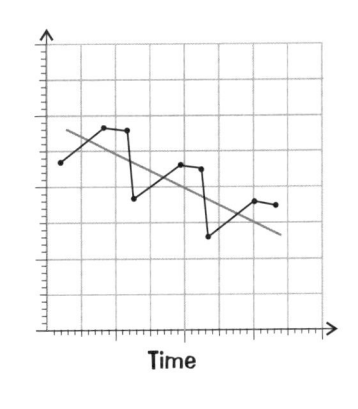

b) Describe the underlying trend for each chart.

i) .... ii) .... iii) ....

Q2 A gardener records the temperature in her greenhouse every 2 hours over a 12-hour period. Her results are shown in the table below.

	0900	1100	1300	1500	1700	1900	2100
Temperature (°C)	27	28	30	31.5	30.5	29	28

a) Draw a time series graph to show this data on the grid to the right.

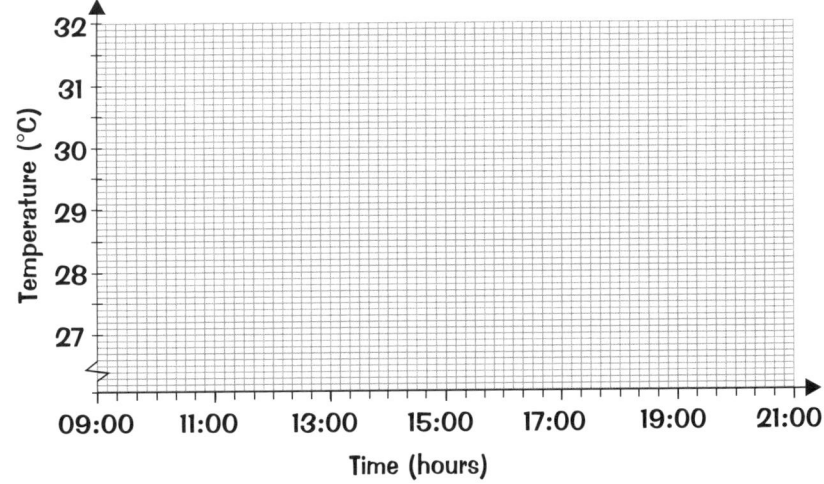

b) Describe the trend of the data between 09:00 and 15:00.

....

c) Describe the trend of the data between 15:00 and 21:00.

....

Section Two — Tabulation and Representation

More Diagrams, Problems and Errors

Diagrams can sometimes be misleading... things can start to get really confusing when you try to do fancy things like make your bar chart 3D or paint a portrait of the Queen's face on your pie chart...

Q1 The diagram shows information about two large regions of the world.
Information includes energy used, income, etc.
The key shows the value of each symbol.

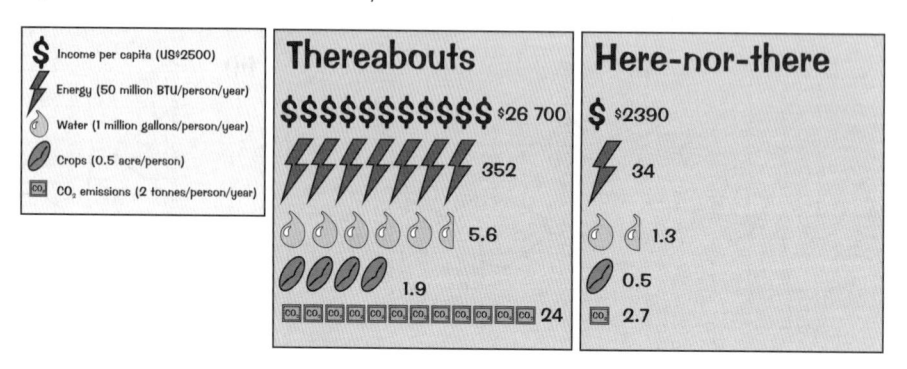

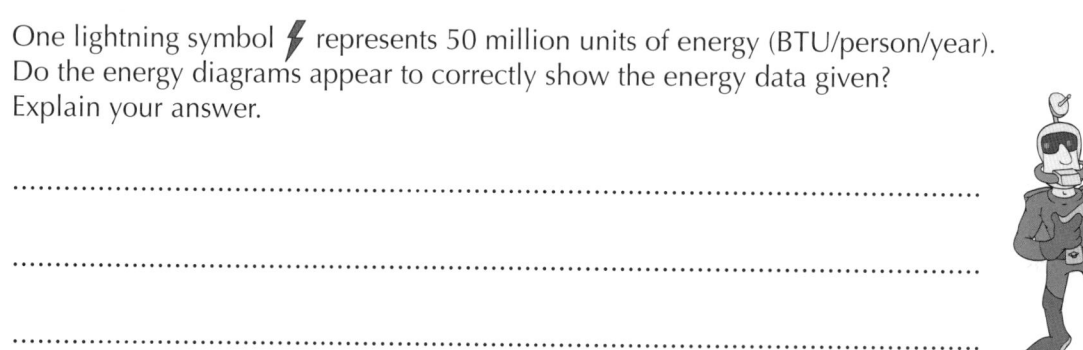

Key:
- $ Income per capita (US$2500)
- ⚡ Energy (50 million BTU/person/year)
- 💧 Water (1 million gallons/person/year)
- 🌱 Crops (0.5 acre/person)
- CO_2 emissions (2 tonnes/person/year)

Thereabouts
- $$$$$$$$$$$ $26 700
- ⚡⚡⚡⚡⚡⚡⚡ 352
- 💧💧💧💧💧 5.6
- 🌱🌱🌱🌱 1.9
- CO_2 × 10 24

Here-nor-there
- $ $2390
- ⚡ 34
- 💧💧 1.3
- 🌱 0.5
- CO_2 2.7

One lightning symbol ⚡ represents 50 million units of energy (BTU/person/year).
Do the energy diagrams appear to correctly show the energy data given?
Explain your answer.

....

....

....

Q2 The graph below shows average monthly temperatures for the months April to August.

a) Jane thinks that the temperature for April has been plotted incorrectly. Do you agree? Explain your answer.

....

....

....

b) The *x*-axis is unevenly scaled.
What effect does this have on the graph?

....

....

SECTION TWO — TABULATION AND REPRESENTATION

More Diagrams, Problems and Errors

Q3 Fred practised taking free kicks at a target goal. In each practice, he took 100 shots. In the first practice, he hit the target 40 times. In the second practice, he hit the target 80 times. Fred draws 4 different diagrams to show how his shooting has improved.

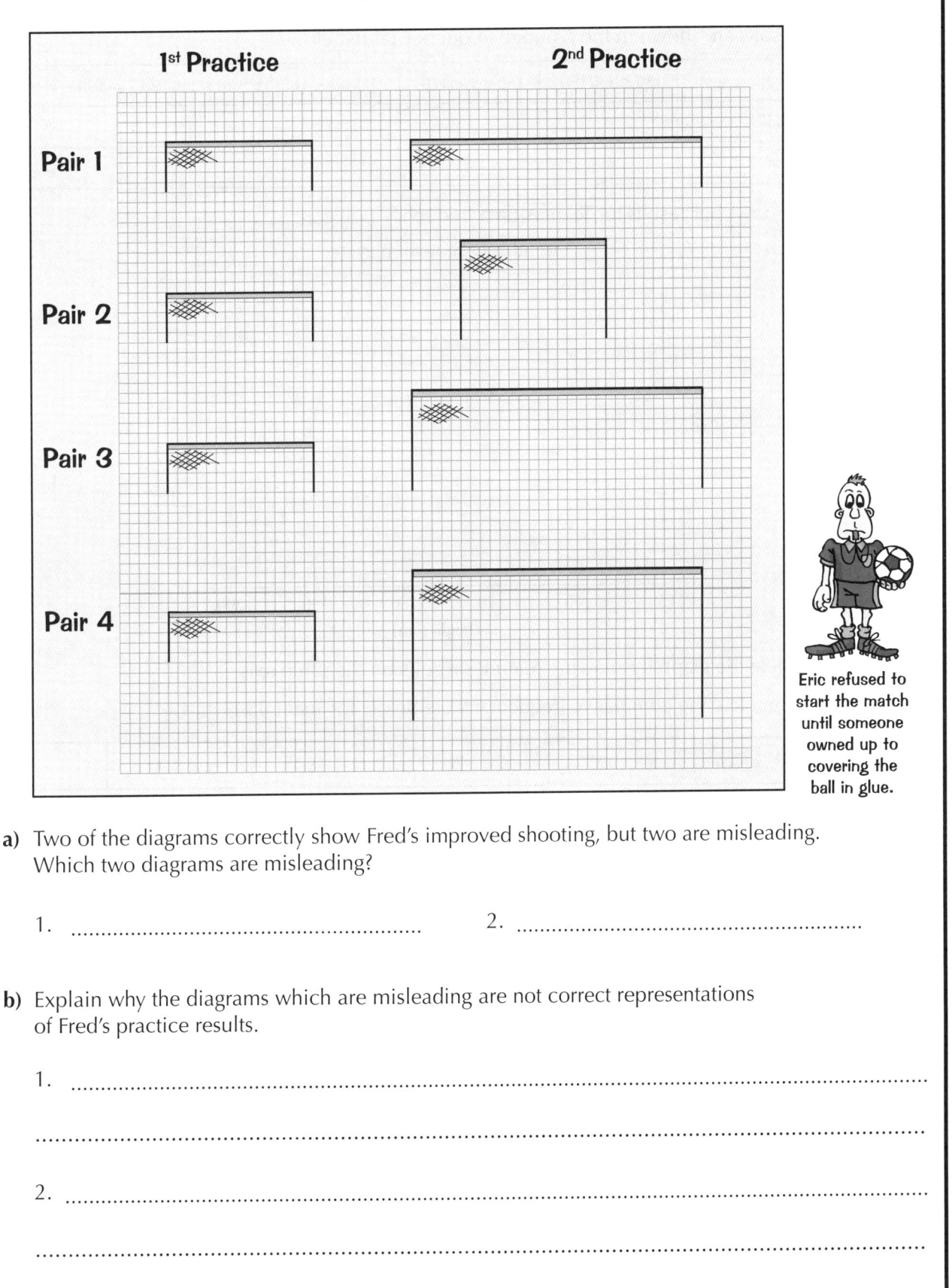

Eric refused to start the match until someone owned up to covering the ball in glue.

a) Two of the diagrams correctly show Fred's improved shooting, but two are misleading. Which two diagrams are misleading?

1. .... 2. ....

b) Explain why the diagrams which are misleading are not correct representations of Fred's practice results.

1. ....
....

2. ....
....

SECTION TWO — TABULATION AND REPRESENTATION

Mixed Questions

Now that you've worked through all the questions in Section Two, here are some more just for you...

Q1 Anna measures the heights (in cm) of players on two different school football teams. Her results are shown in the grouped frequency table below:

Height, x (cm)	$150 \leq x < 160$	$160 \leq x < 170$	$170 \leq x < 180$	$180 \leq x < 190$	$190 \leq x < 200$
Team A	0	1	2	7	1
Team B	1	4	5	1	0

Anna shows her results for Team A on a frequency polygon:

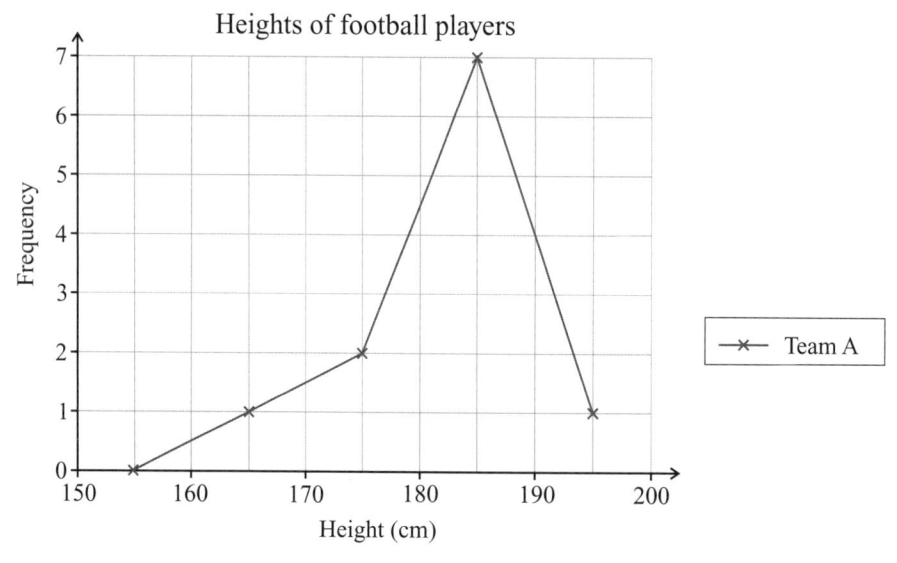

a) Complete the graph by showing Team B's results on the same axis.

b) i) Complete the cumulative frequency table below for Team B's results.

Height, x (cm)	$x < 160$	$x < 170$	$x < 180$	$x < 190$	$x < 200$
Cumulative Frequency	1	5			

ii) Draw a cumulative frequency polygon for Team B's results on the grid below.

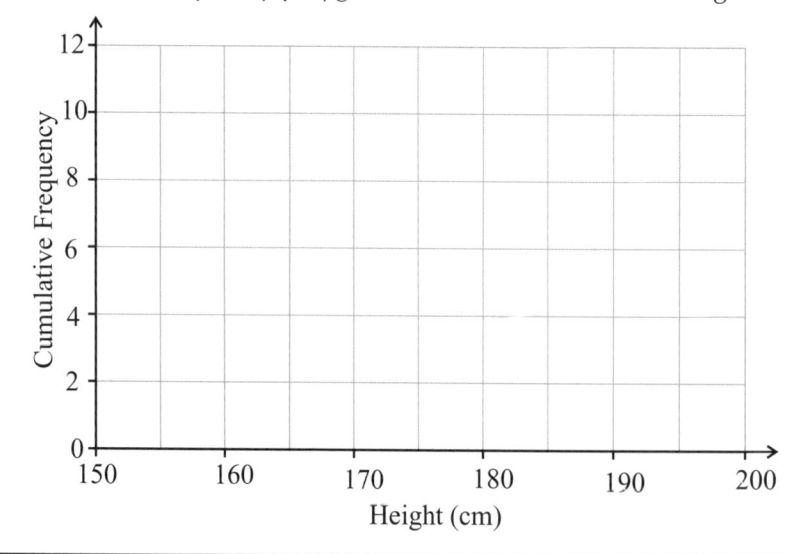

Mixed Questions

Q2 A group of 20 pupils were asked to estimate the length (l) of a straight line without measuring it. The actual length was 10 cm.

The results in centimetres are shown below.

| 10.6 | 9.3 | 9.4 | 11.8 | 11.7 | 8.5 | 9.6 | 6.7 | 7.0 | 10.5 |
| 11.8 | 6.2 | 8.3 | 9.7 | 8.7 | 9.6 | 7.6 | 10.7 | 10.0 | 7.1 |

a) Using the results above, complete this grouped frequency table:

Length (l) cm	Frequency
$6 < l \leq 7$	
$7 < l \leq 8$	
$8 < l \leq 9$	
$9 < l \leq 10$	
$10 < l \leq 11$	
$11 < l \leq 12$	
Total	20

b) State one advantage and one disadvantage of recording this data in a grouped frequency table.

Advantage: ....

....

Disadvantage: ....

....

c) Use the data to draw a histogram on the grid below.

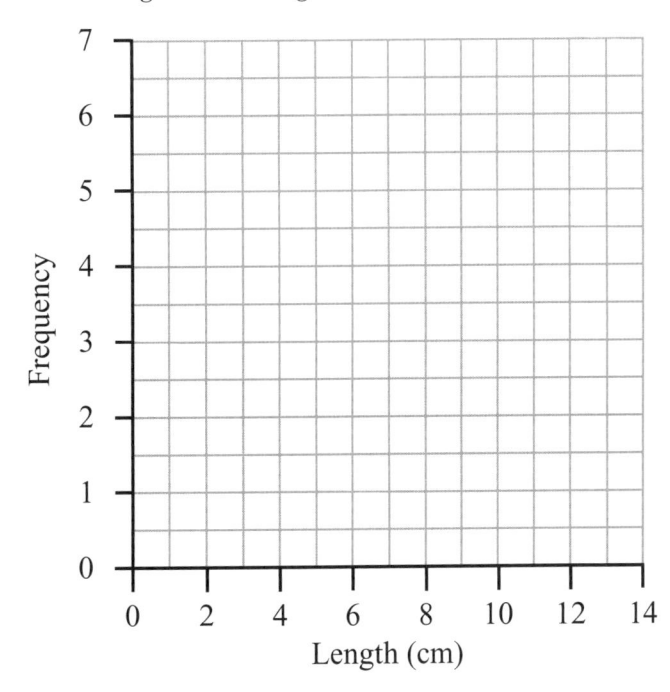

SECTION TWO — TABULATION AND REPRESENTATION

Mean, Median and Mode

Make sure you know the difference between MEAN, MEDIAN AND MODE, and how to work them out. You've got plenty of practice here, so get stuck in.

Q1 Find the mean of each of the sets of data below. If necessary, round your answers to 1 decimal place:

a) 13, 15, 11, 12, 16, 13, 11, 9 = ...

b) 16, 13, 2, 15, 0, 9 = ...

c) 80, 70, 80, 50, 60, 70, 90, 60, 50, 70, 70 = ...

Remember the formula for the mean = total of data values ÷ number of data values.

Q2 These are the heights of fifteen 16-year-olds.

162 cm	156 cm	174 cm	148 cm
152 cm	139 cm	167 cm	134 cm
157 cm	163 cm	149 cm	134 cm
158 cm	172 cm	146 cm

Put the data in order of size for median questions — then it's easy to find the middle value by crossing off numbers from each end.

What is the median height? Write your answer in the shaded box.

To find the mode, put the data in order of size first — then it's easier to see which number you've got most of.

Q3 The midday temperatures in °C on 10 summer days in England were:

25, 18, 23, 19, 23, 24, 23, 18, 20, 19

What was the modal midday temperature?

....

Q4 On a large box of matches it says "Average contents 240 matches". I counted the number of matches in ten boxes. These are the results:

241 244 236 240 239 242 237 239 239 236

Is the label on the box correct? Use the mean, median and mode for the numbers of matches to explain your answer.

....

....

Mean, Median and Mode — Discrete Data

If you've collected discrete data and recorded it in a frequency table, you can still analyse it by calculating the mean, median and mode.

Q1 For a set of data, $\Sigma xf = 396$ and $\Sigma f = 12$.
Calculate the mean for this data set.

Mean $(\bar{x}) = \Sigma xf / \Sigma f$

....

Q2 Every time Roger plays golf he keeps a record of his score on the first hole.
The table below shows his last 120 scores.

Score	3	4	5	6	7	8
Frequency	2	15	38	34	23	8
Score × Frequency						

a) What is the modal score?

....

b) Fill in the third row of the table.

c) What is the total of Roger's last 120 scores?

....

d) What is his mean score?

....

Q3 The ages of a group of 30 children in a playground are given in the tally chart below:

Age	1	2	3	4	5	6
Tally	II	IIII	III	IIII	IIII IIII	IIII I

a) What is the mean age? Give the answer to the nearest whole number of years.

....

....

b) What is the median?

....

Mean, Median and Mode — Grouped Data

Finding the three 'M's for grouped data can be a pain in the... side.
It's really important for the exam though, so practise with these questions.

Q1 In a survey of test results in a French class at Blugdon High, these grades were achieved by the 23 pupils:

(grade) score	(E) 31-40	(D) 41-50	(C) 51-60	(B) 61-70
frequency	4	7	8	4

The **MID-INTERVAL VALUES** are just what they sound like — the middle of the group.

a) Write down the mid-interval values for each of the groups.

....

b) Calculate an estimate for the mean value.

....

....

Q2 This table shows times for two teams of swimmers, the Dolphins and the Sharks.

Dolphins				**Sharks**			
Time interval (seconds)	Frequency	Mid-interval value	Frequency × Mid-interval value	Time interval (seconds)	Frequency	Mid-interval value	Frequency × Mid-interval value
$14 \leq t < 20$	3	17	151	$14 \leq t < 20$	6	17	102
$20 \leq t < 26$	7	23	161	$20 \leq t < 26$	15	23	345
$26 \leq t < 32$	15			$26 \leq t < 32$	33		
$32 \leq t < 38$	32			$32 \leq t < 38$	59		
$38 \leq t < 44$	45			$38 \leq t < 44$	20		
$44 \leq t < 50$	30			$44 \leq t < 50$	8		
$50 \leq t < 56$	5			$50 \leq t < 56$	2		

a) Complete the table. Write in all the **mid-interval** values and the **frequency × mid-interval** values.

b) Calculate an estimate of the mean time for each team.
Give the answer to the nearest 0.1 seconds.

....

....

....

c) What is the modal class for the dolphins?

....

SECTION THREE — DATA ANALYSIS

Mean, Median and Mode — Grouped Data

Q3 Dean is carrying out a survey for his Geography coursework. He asked 80 people how many miles they drove their car last year to the nearest thousand. He has started filling in a grouped frequency table to show his results.

No. of Miles (thousands)	1 - 10	11 - 20	21 - 30	31 - 40	41 - 50	51 - 60	61 - 70	71 - 80	81 - 90	91 - 100
No. of Cars	2	3	5	19	16	14	10	7		

a) Complete Dean's table using the following information:

   81 245,   82 675,   90 159,   90 569

b) Write down the modal class. ....

c) Which class contains the median number of miles driven?   ....

Q4 The heights of 11 African elephants are recorded in the table below.

Height (cm)	Frequency
$300 < x \leq 310$	1
$310 < x \leq 320$	3
$320 < x \leq 330$	3
$330 < x \leq 340$	4

This is a really tricky question so don't worry if you find it hard. Just work through it step-by-step and make sure you use the handy hints.

a) In which group is the median height?
   Hint: Remember the median's overall position number is (n +1)/2.

   ....

b) Show that the median is the 2nd value in the group.
   Hint: The position in group = overall position – number of positions below median group.

   ....

c) What is this position as a proportion?
   Hint: The proportion of way through group = position in group / number of values in group.

   ....

d) Multiply your answer to part c) by the class width of the median group.

   ....

e) Work out an estimate for the median height using your answer to part d).
   Hint: Add part d) to the median group's lower class boundary.

   ....

SECTION THREE — DATA ANALYSIS

Choosing the Best Average

Make sure you understand the differences between the mean, median and mode so that you know which one to use for a particular data set...

Q1 What average should be used for qualitative data?

....

Q2 A manufacturer tested the lifetime of a particular type of light bulb so that he could confidently state how many hours they lasted. The results for eight such light bulbs are as follows:

| 3090 | 2400 | 2010 | 2520 | 90 | 2620 | 2800 | 2550 |

    a) Which average should he use?

....

    b) Which average would be the least useful, and why?

....

....

    c) What should the manufacturer do to be more sure of his statement?

....

Averages — shedding light on your data...

Q3 State the most appropriate average (mean, median or mode) for working out each of the following:

    a) A cricketer's batting average. ....

    b) The most popular type of music at a school. ....

    c) The average number of people visiting a theme park every day in August, including the August Bank holiday when the theme park puts on a special event. ....

You need to remember when it's best to use the mean, median and mode — and why...

SECTION THREE — DATA ANALYSIS

Range, Quartiles and Percentiles

Remember to put the data in order from <u>lowest to highest</u> (ascending order) before you work out where the quartiles or percentiles come in a list.

Q1 The weights (in g) of 9 eggs are:

| 60 | 72 | 58 | 60 | 68 | 69 | 59 | 72 | 54 |

a) What is the range?

....

b) i) Put the data in ascending order.

Position	1	2	3	4	5	6	7	8	9

ii) What is the lower quartile, Q_1?

....

Q2 The following data set shows the number of cars parked in a multi-storey car park at midday on eleven different days in December:

| 690 | 720 | 580 | 590 | 210 | 650 | 640 | 710 | 700 | 750 | 790 |

a) What is the range?

....

Quartiles divide the data into 4 equal groups and percentiles divide it into 100 equal groups.

b) What is the median, Q_2?

....

c) What is the upper quartile, Q_3?

....

Q3 The following data shows the number of appointments not kept at the local doctor's surgery each month for the last eleven months:

| 38 | 52 | 18 | 25 | 32 | 21 | 42 | 23 | 29 | 37 | 24 |

a) What is the upper quartile?

....

b) What is the 50th percentile?

....

SECTION THREE — DATA ANALYSIS

Interquartile Range

*Right, now for some lovely questions on estimating ranges.
I hope you're ready to plot some curves... thrilling stuff this.*

Q1 For the set of whole numbers from 1 to 399 inclusive, what is the interquartile range?

The interquartile range is the difference between the upper quartile and the lower quartile: $Q_3 - Q_1$.

....

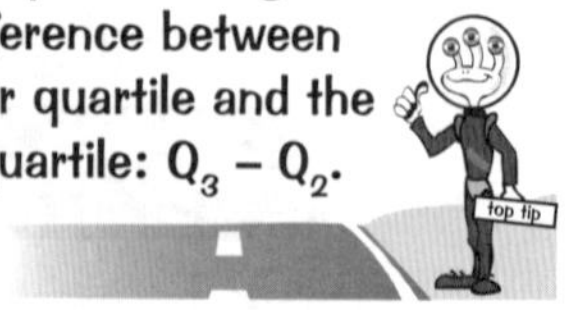

Q2 The graph on the right shows the cumulative frequency curve for the height in cm of 200 sunflowers at 8 weeks old.

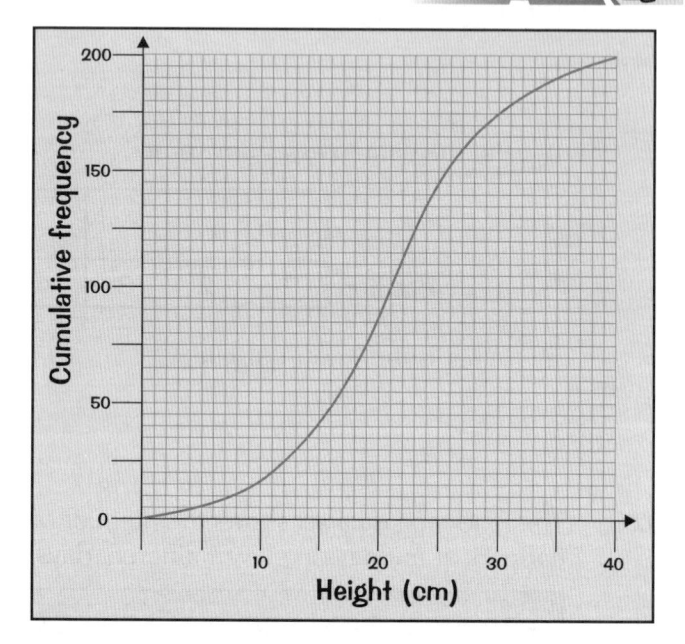

  a) Estimate the median height.

  ....

  b) What is the interquartile range?

  ....

  ....

Q3 The weights (in kg) of a company's employees were taken and recorded in the table below:

Weight (kg)	Freq	Cum freq
w<50	0	0
50≤w<55	3	3
55≤w<60	8	11
60≤w<65	27	38
65≤w<70	32	70
70≤w<75	25	95
75≤w<80	29	124
80≤w<85	35	159
85≤w<90	27	186
90≤w<95	18	204
95≤w<100	6	210

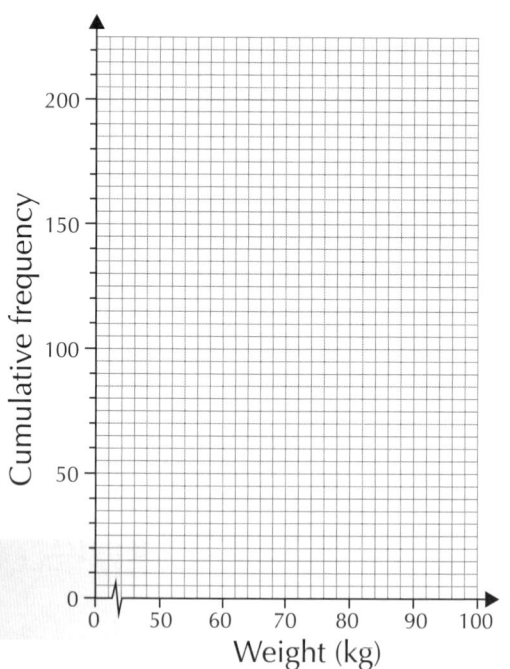

  a) Plot the cumulative frequency curve for the data on the grid above.

  b) Use your graph to find the interquartile range.

....

SECTION THREE — DATA ANALYSIS

Box and Whisker Plots

Hey! Pretty pictures... kind of...

Q1 Describe the skew for each of the following box plots:

a) ....

b) ....

c) ....

Q2 On the grid below, draw a box plot using the following information:

Lowest value = 1   Lower quartile = 17   Median = 24

Range = 38   Upper quartile = 28

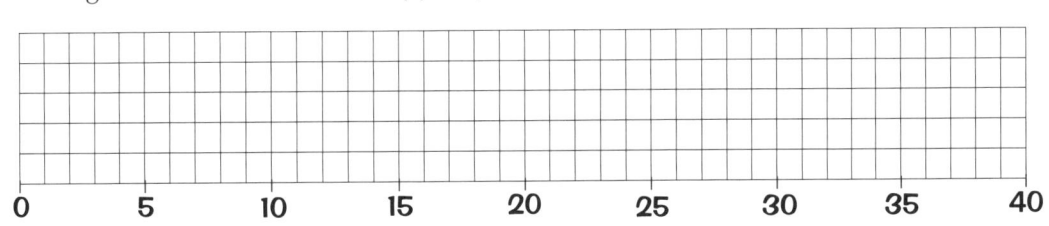

A box and whisker plot is sometimes just called a box plot.

Q3 The box and whisker plot below shows the age distribution of people in a small village.

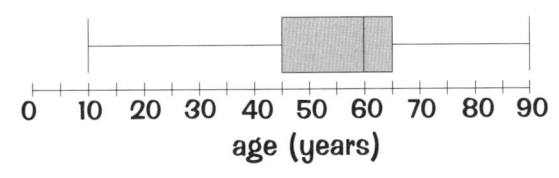

a) Write down the median age. ....

b) Work out the interquartile range.

....

c) Describe the skew of the data set.

....

SECTION THREE — DATA ANALYSIS

Comparing Data Sets

You can use averages and measures of spread to compare data sets.

Q1 A summary of two batsmen's scores for a cricket season is shown in the table below.

a) Which batsman had the best batting average?
Explain your choice.

....

....

	A	B
Mean	48	65
Median	47	51
Range	164	130

b) Give another comparison between the batsmen's scores.

....

....

Q2 The employees of a company usually travel to work by car or by bike.
The box plot below shows the journey times (in minutes) for those who travel by car.

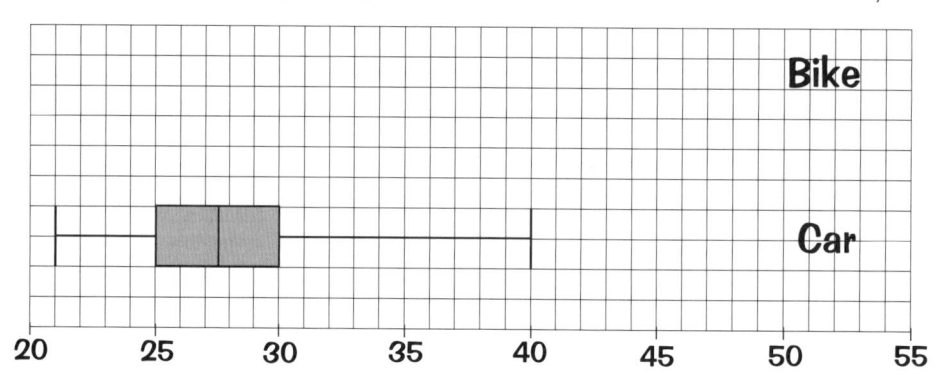

The table gives information about the journey times (in minutes) for employees who cycle to work.

	Minimum	Q_1	Q_2	Q_3	Maximum
Bike	33	37	43	45	48

a) Use this data to draw a box plot to show the distribution of bike times on the grid above.

b) Describe **two differences** between the distributions.

1. ....

2. ....

SECTION THREE — DATA ANALYSIS

Index Numbers and Crude Rates

You've got to know all about index numbers (they're really useful if your data includes prices).

Q1 The value of a piece of land increased over one year, as shown:

Year	2007	2008
Value (£)	25 000	30 000

$$\text{Index Number} = \frac{\text{value}}{\text{value in base year}} \times 100$$

a) Using 2007 as the base year, calculate the index number for 2008.

....

b) By what percentage did the value of the land increase between 2007 and 2008?

....

Q2 Here are the index numbers showing the price of a particular model of car since it was launched in the year 2005:

Year	2005	2006	2007
Index	100	108	112

a) Which year is the base year?

....

b) If the car first came onto the market for £26 000, what was the price of the car in 2007?

....

....

If you're doing AQA then you've got to know crude rates inside out as well — so enjoy. ☺

Q3 Last year the number of deaths in Wentwell was 432. If Wentwell had a population of 28 600, what was the crude death rate last year?

....

....

The crude birth/death rate is the number of births/deaths per thousand of the population.

Q4 The number of births in Bournville in 2008 was 321. If the population in 2008 was 15 000, what was the crude birth rate that year?

....

SECTION THREE — DATA ANALYSIS

Time Series

Time series graphs can be really useful if you want to make predictions for the future. But first it's best to plot moving averages to make your trend line more accurate.

Q1 For the following set of data, calculate 3-point moving averages:

60, 65, 55, 57, 63, 55, 62, 60, 58

Q2 A shoe shop recorded the total number of pairs of shoes sold every 3 months from January 2007 to December 2009. The information is recorded in the table below.

	Jan-Mar	Apr-Jun	Jul-Sep	Oct-Dec
2007	2150	2270	1950	2480
2008	2850	2820	2780	3110
2009	3250	2950	3300	3440

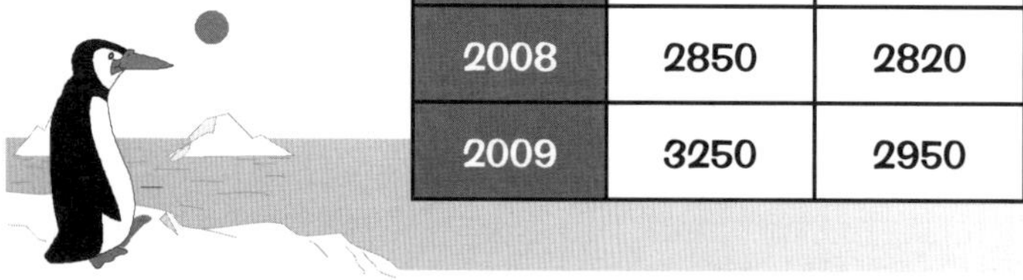

Remember to plot at the mid-point of the time interval.

a) Draw a time series graph on the grid below to show this data.

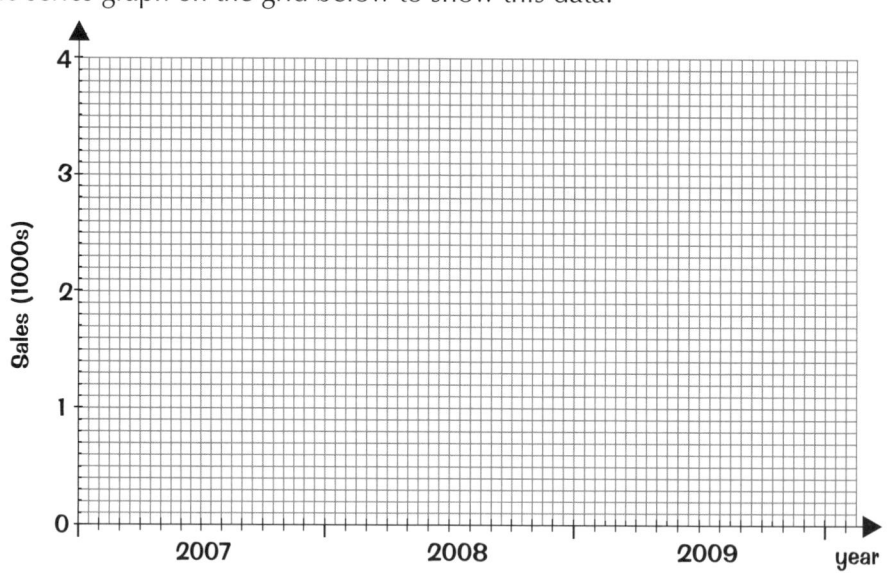

b) Draw on a trend line.

c) Use the trend line to predict the number of pairs of shoes sold between Jan and Mar 2010.

SECTION THREE — DATA ANALYSIS

Time Series and Output Gap Charts

Q1 The table below shows sales at a bakery over three weeks.

Week	1					2					3				
Day	M	Tu	W	Th	F	M	Tu	W	Th	F	M	Tu	W	Th	F
Sales (£)	100	130	120	80	110	105	135	130	90	110	110	140	140	100	115
Moving Average			108	109											

a) Calculate the remaining 5-point moving averages for the data. Put your answers in the table.

b) Plot the moving averages on the grid below and draw a trend line through the points.

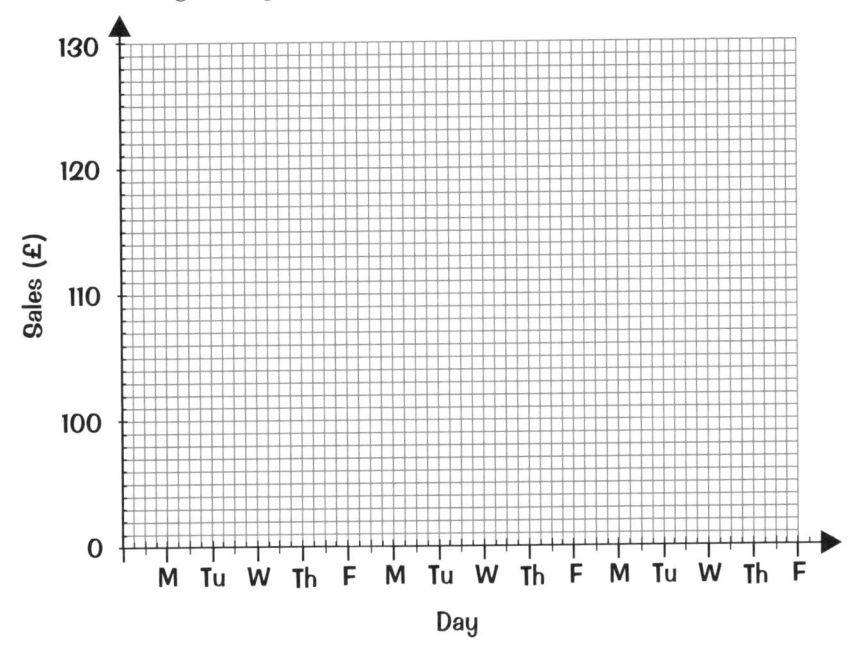

Q2 Here is an output gap chart for the small state of Richenstein:

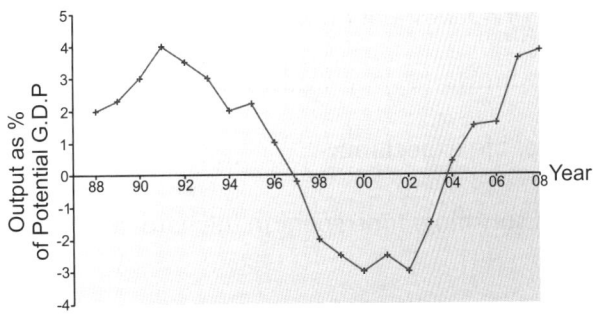

a) Describe the state of the Richenstein economy between 2004 and 2008.

....

b) What happens to prices of goods in a boom?

....

c) Explain why unemployment started to rise in Richenstein in 1997.

....

Section Three — Data Analysis

Correlation

Two variables can be positively correlated, negatively correlated or not correlated at all.

Q1 What does correlation mean?

....

Q2 Describe the correlation shown by the following graphs.
(Make sure you answer in terms of the variables involved).

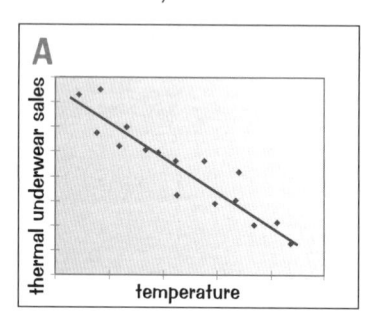

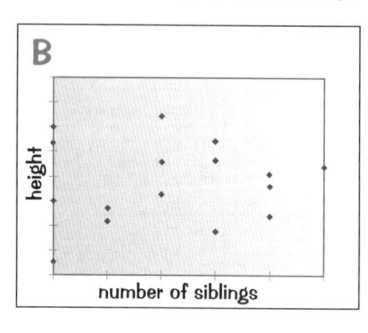

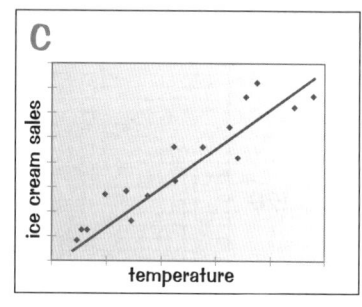

A thermal underwear sales vs temperature

B height vs number of siblings

C ice cream sales vs temperature

A ....

B ....

C ....

Q3 For each pair of variables below, state what type of correlation (**positive, negative** or **none**) you'd expect if you plotted them against each other.

a) Outside temperature, number of visitors to the zoo ....

b) Number of hours spent on homework, number of hours spent watching television

....

c) Shoe size, life expectancy ....

d) Hours of sunshine, time spent in the garden ....

Causality means that a change in one variable causes a change in the other variable.

Q4 State which of the following pairs of variables, if any, have a causal link. (Write **yes** or **no**.)

a) Speed of car, stopping distance ....

b) Temperature outside, heating bills ....

c) GCSE Mathematics score, height ....

Section Three — Data Analysis

Correlation

The following questions refer to the scatter diagrams below:

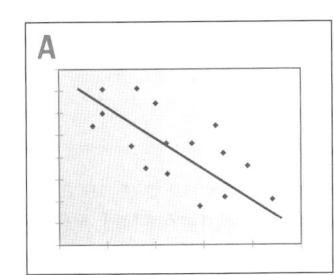

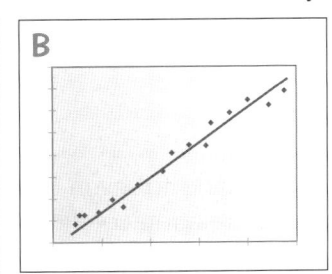

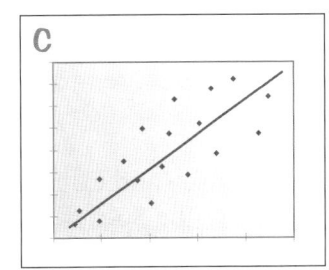

A   B   C

Q5 State which of the scatter diagrams above has a:

a) strong positive correlation ....

b) weak negative correlation ....

c) weak positive correlation ....

Q6 The table below shows the ages of a sample of boys and the number of packets of crisps they eat in an average week.

Age	10	7	12	16	13	12	15	11	8	15
Packets of crisps	3	10	1	5	12	7	8	4	2	3

a) Plot this data on the grid below.

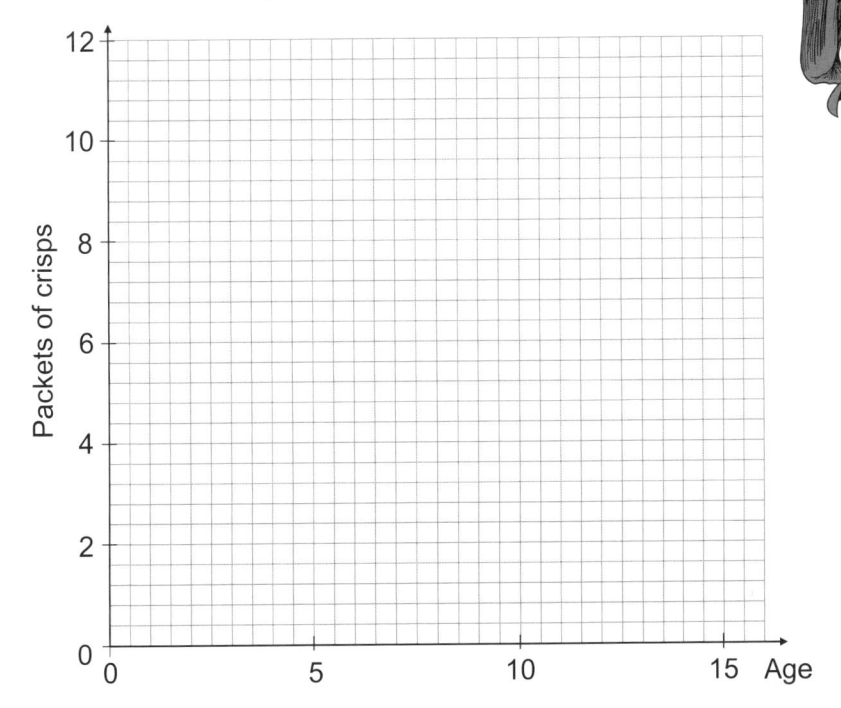

b) Is there any correlation? If so, draw a line of best fit.

SECTION THREE — DATA ANALYSIS

Correlation

Q7 (AQA only) What range of values can Spearman's rank correlation coefficient take?

....

Q8 (AQA only) Judges Benchley and Court awarded marks to seven competitors taking part in a gymnastics competition. The Spearman's rank correlation coefficient was calculated to be 0.93 (to 2 d.p.).

Comment on what the Spearman's rank correlation coefficient above means.

....

....

Q9 A van driver wanted to know if the load he carried affected the van's diesel consumption, so he recorded the details for several long trips he made:

Load (tonnes)	0.5	2.6	7.0	2.8	5.0	7.2	6.0	1.3	3.6	4.4
Miles per litre	6.9	6.3	4.3	5.9	5.2	4.6	5.0	6.7	5.9	5.6

a) Plot the data on the grid below.

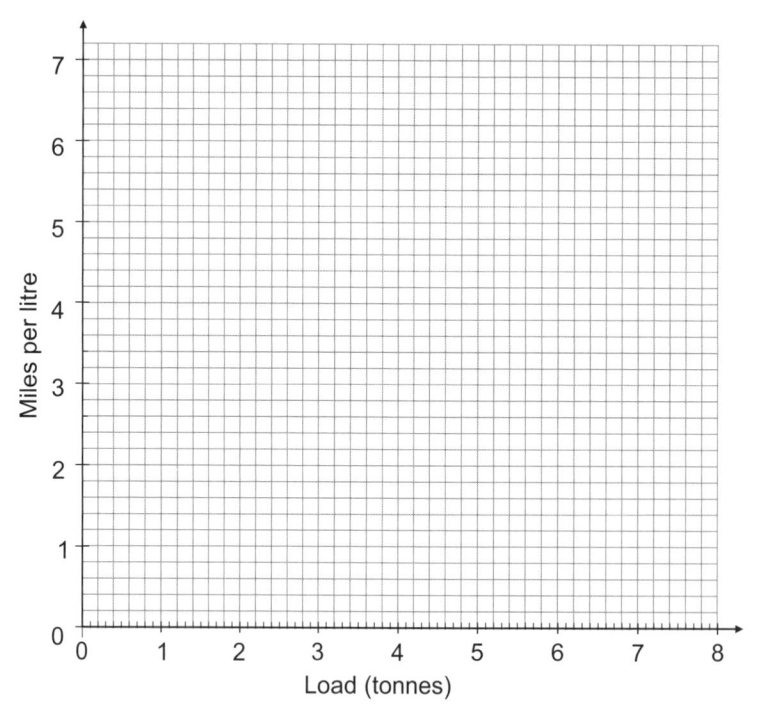

b) Draw a line of best fit.

c) Describe the correlation shown, referring to the variables involved.

....

Section Three — Data Analysis

Interpolation and Extrapolation

You can use scatter diagrams to predict unknown values, so have a go with these questions...

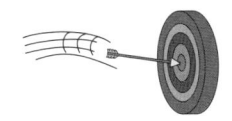

Q1 a) Define the term "interpolation".

　..

b) Give a disadvantage of using extrapolation.

　..

Q2 The number of tickets sold and the associated bar takings for some pub gigs are tabulated below:

Number of tickets sold	45	68	24	38	57	63	60
Bar takings (£)	340	560	150	290	510	600	550

a) Plot this data on the grid below and draw a line of best fit.

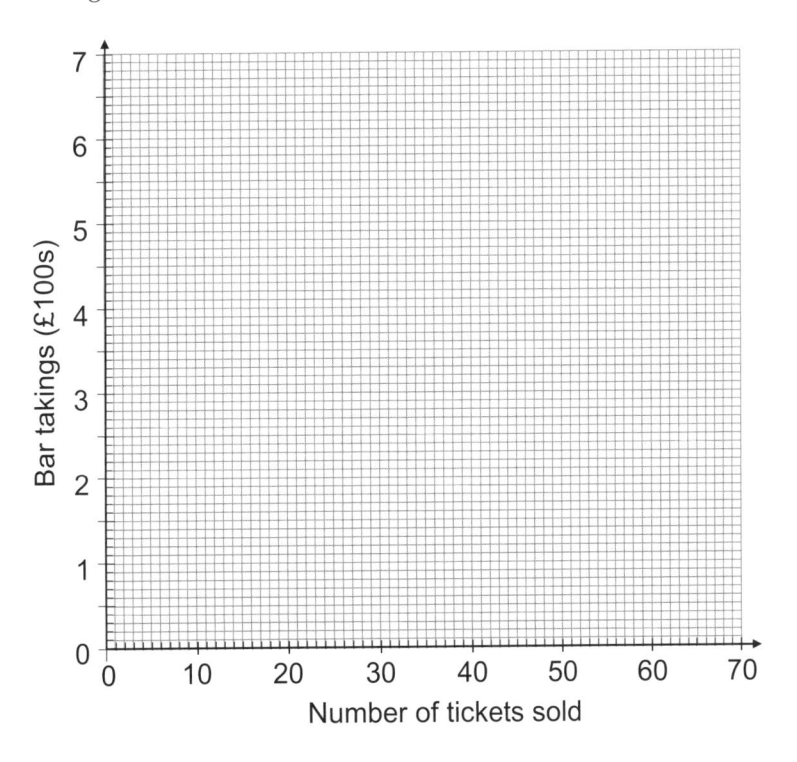

b) If just 30 tickets are sold, how much money is the bar likely to take?

　..

c) The maximum number of people allowed in the pub is 70. Estimate the bar takings then.

　..

SECTION THREE — DATA ANALYSIS

Estimation of Population

A lot of populations are too big, or too hard to track down, to be able to do a census. So you can use samples to make estimates about a population.

Q1 Hazel has a large number of slugs in her garden. To find out what type of slug they are, she needs to know their lengths. She measures ten slugs in total, with the following results:

| 12 cm | 14 cm | 12.5 cm | 11.5 cm | 13.5 cm |
| 13 cm | 12 cm | 10 cm | 11 cm | 13 cm |

Use Hazel's measurements to estimate the mean length of the slugs in her garden.

....

Q2 A farmer has **30** equally populated henhouses. He collected and counted the eggs from **six** of these houses on the same day, with the following results:

| 37 | 42 | 35 | 47 | 42 | 37 |

a) How many eggs, on average, does each of these henhouses yield?

....

b) How many eggs would the farmer expect to get altogether each day?

....

Q3 Some students at Braggleton University conducted an opinion poll to find out if their fellow students approved of top-up fees. They asked **100** students from each of two year groups. The results are tabulated below.

	Yes	No	Don't know
1st Years	10	80	10
2nd Years	15	80	5

A sample needs to be big enough to accurately represent the population.

a) Based on the data in the table, estimate what percentage of students agreed with the introduction of top-up fees.

....

b) How could this estimate have been improved?

....

c) What do the majority of students think?

....

SECTION THREE — DATA ANALYSIS

Mixed Questions

If you still have loads of topics from Section Three swimming round your head then you can put them to good use by trying these mixed questions.

Q1 120 people were asked how long, on average, they spend reading the Sunday newspaper. The cumulative frequency graph below shows the results.

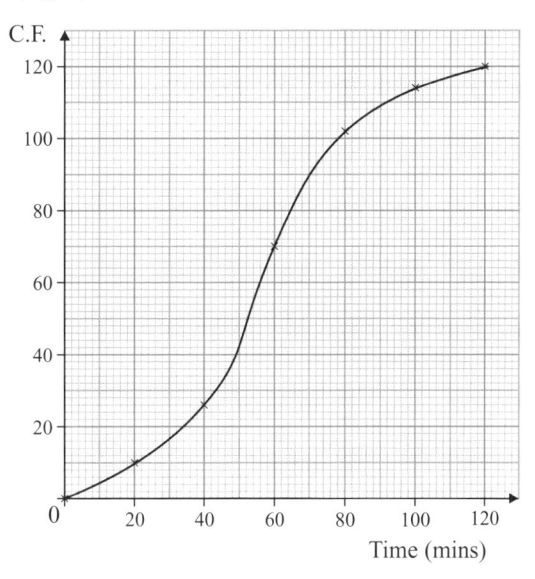

a) Use the graph to estimate how many people spent 50 minutes or less reading the newspaper.

....

b) Use the graph to estimate the median time taken reading the Sunday newspaper.

....

Q2 The members of Scoresdale Sports Club go out each weekend to try different sports. One week they went karting at a local circuit and recorded all their lap times. Dave's lap times were 67, 64, 112, 69, 74, and 71 seconds.

a) i) Work out the median for Dave's lap times.

....

ii) What is an advantage of using the median for this data set.

....

b) i) Work out the range of Dave's lap times.

....

ii) Give one criticism of using the range as a measure of spread for this data.

....

SECTION THREE — DATA ANALYSIS

Mixed Questions

Q3 A meteorology station records the temperature, T (°C), to an accuracy of one tenth of a degree at the same time on consecutive days.

Day	1	2	3	4	5
T (°C)	5.4	6.2	4.0	4.8	5.6

The first three-point moving average is 5.2 °C.

a) Calculate the next two three-point moving averages.

i) ....

ii) ....

A weather forecaster collects data from 10 different meteorology stations.
The table below shows the average weekly temperature, T (°C) and the total weekly rainfall, R (mm), for each of these stations for one week.

Total weekly rainfall, R (mm)	14	7	21	10	8	15	18	23	14	16
Average weekly temperature, T (°C)	13.4	15.7	11.0	16.2	14.3	14.8	12.5	9.8	11.2	14.1

b) i) Draw a scatter diagram on the grid below to show the data above.

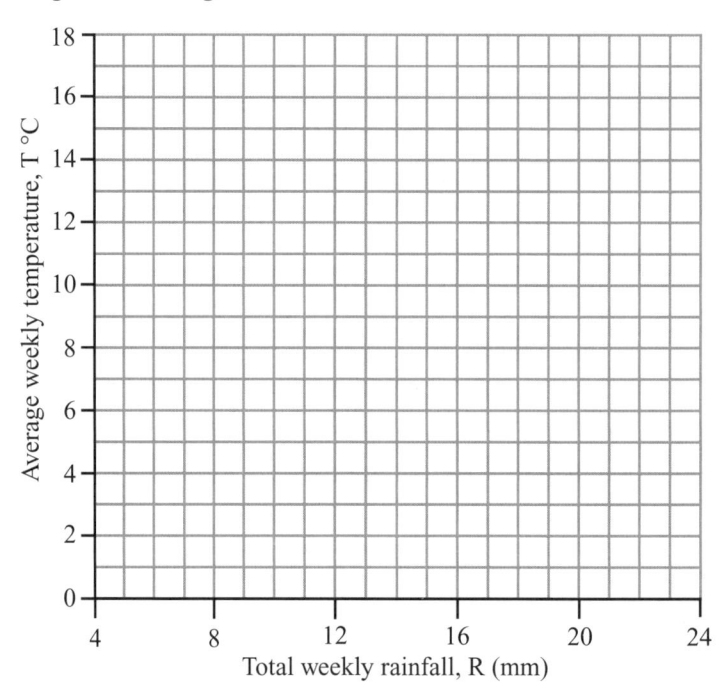

ii) The mean weekly temperature is 13.3 °C. Calculate the mean weekly rainfall.

....

c) i) Draw a line of best fit on the scatter diagram.
Hint: Make sure the line of best fit goes through the mean of both variables.

ii) Describe the correlation shown, referring to the variables shown.

....

SECTION THREE — DATA ANALYSIS

SECTION FOUR — PROBABILITY

Probability

Remember: the probability of any event happening must lie between 0 and 1 — the more likely an event is to happen, the closer its probability will be to 1.

Q1 This is a probability scale:

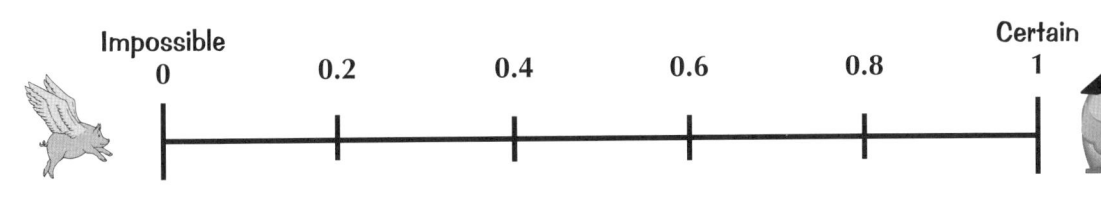

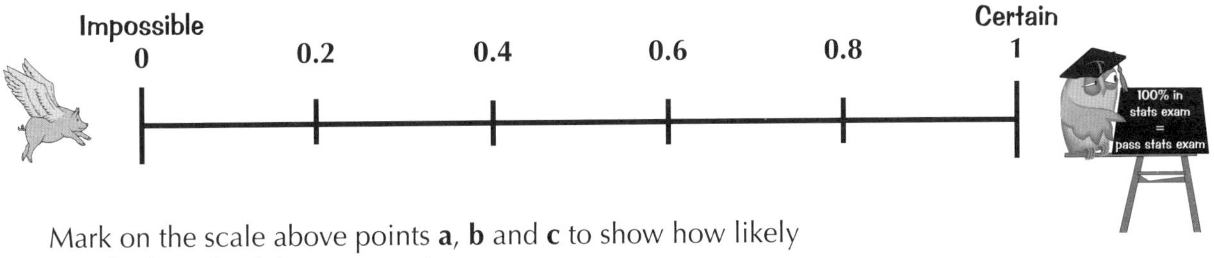

Impossible 0 — 0.2 — 0.4 — 0.6 — 0.8 — Certain 1

Mark on the scale above points **a**, **b** and **c** to show how likely you think each of these events is:

a) A van that is less than a year old will break down in the next year.

b) A van that is 50 years old will break down in the next year.

c) A van that is 10 years old will break down in the next year.

Q2 Christina says that she has a probability of 1.4 of passing her GCSE Statistics exam. Explain why this isn't possible.

....

Q3 Two goats, Glenda and Gertrude, have a sprint race. If both goats finish the race, there are three possible outcomes. What are they?

1. .... 2. .... 3. ....

Q4 For each of these spinners, decide the following:

i) which number is **most** likely to be spun.
ii) which number is **least** likely to be spun.

a) 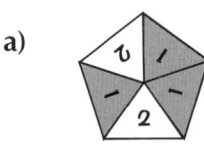 i) .... ii) ....

b)  i) .... ii) ....

c) 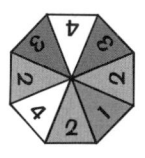 i) .... ii) ....

d)  i) .... ii) ....

SECTION FOUR — PROBABILITY

Probability

These probability questions can be a tricky business. All you're really interested in is the number of ways an event can happen, compared to the total number of things that can happen. Remember that — and you're sorted.

Q5 David has **10** marbles in his pocket. He wants to show his friend his favourite marble. If he picks **one** marble at random from his pocket, what is the probability that it's his favourite?

....

Q6 The managers of a ski resort are trying to improve the safety of the resort. Last month 50% of those reporting an injury were between 18 and 24 years old, 36% were between 25 and 50 years old and 14% were over 50.

Assuming the above figures represent a typical week, answer this question:

What's the probability of someone who reports an injury being between 25 and 50 years old?

....

Q7 Dorothy throws a **standard dice**. What is the probability that she will get:

a) an odd number? ....

b) 2? ....

c) an even number? ....

d) a number equal to 3 or more? ....

Q8 **24** runners taking part in a marathon all have an equal probability of winning. Eight of the runners are women and the rest are men.

a) What is the probability of a woman winning the race? ....

b) What is the probability of a man winning the race? ....

Only 12 of the runners are wearing tracksuits.

c) What is the probability of a person wearing a tracksuit winning the race? ....

Q9 Richard has been given a packet of mixed sweets. If he picks **one** sweet at random, he has a probability of **0.25** of picking a mint-flavoured sweet.

How many sweets are in the packet if there are **seven** mint-flavoured sweets?

....

Section Four — Probability

Probability

Q10 A river is likely to burst its bank after heavy rainfall. Heavy rainfall always happens once a year. In the last 40 years, House A has flooded 8 times.

a) What is the probability that House A will flood if there is heavy rainfall? ....

House B is closer to the river and has flooded 22 times.

b) What is the probability that House B will flood. ....

Q11 A two-way table showing the results of a traffic survey is shown below.

Type of vehicle	Red	Blue	Green	White	Total
Car	12	12	5	3	32
Lorry	2	1	0	11	
Motorbike	1	2	0	1	
Total					

a) Complete the table.

b) How many vehicles were counted altogether in the survey? ....

c) A vehicle is selected at random from the survey. Find the probability that the vehicle is:

   i) a red lorry ....

   ii) a car ....

   iii) a green motorbike ....

   iv) blue ....

Q12 In a lottery 50 balls are numbered 1 to 50. A single ball is chosen at random and the person with a ticket that matches that number wins.

a) What is the probability of the ball being an odd number?

....

b) What is the probability of the ball being greater than 30?

....

If something is random then all the outcomes are equally likely.

c) Jane buys tickets for 5 different balls. What is the probability she will win?

....

SECTION FOUR — PROBABILITY

Sample Space Diagrams

All these lovely diagrams — it's almost like art. And they're useful too. Diagrams make it much easier to work out probabilities as they show all the possible outcomes. So it might help to draw one even if you're not asked to.

Q1 Circle the correct sample space for an eight-sided dice numbered 1-8.

  1, 2, 3, 4, 5, 6, 7, 8   1, 2, 3, 4, 5, 6   1, 2, 3

Q2 A standard dice is rolled and the spinner below is spun. Complete the sample space diagram on the right to show all the possible outcomes.

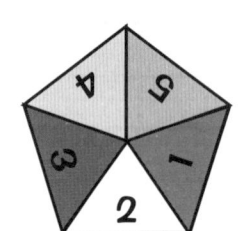

	Spinner				
	1	2	3	4	5
Dice 1	1,1	1,2	1,3	1,4	1,5
2					
3					
4					
5					
6					

AQA only

Q3 Roy has started to draw a Cartesian grid to work out the possible outcomes of throwing a standard green dice and a standard yellow dice.

a) Complete the grid to show all possible outcomes.

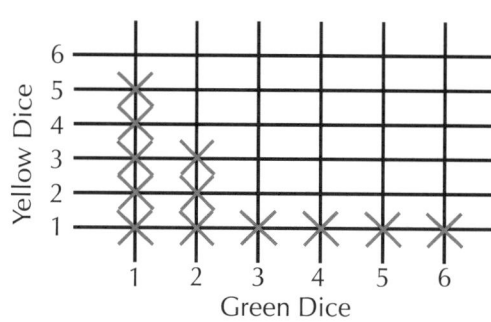

b) How many outcomes are there in total? ....

c) Write down the probability of:

  i) getting a 2 on the green dice with any number on the yellow dice. ....

  ii) getting two numbers that are both less than 5. ....

  iii) getting two odd numbers. ....

SECTION FOUR — PROBABILITY

Venn Diagrams

If you're doing the **AQA** course and you love circles, this page is for you. It's all about Venn diagrams. Each circle represents a set of data with the number inside showing how many things are in that set. Numbers in the bit where two circles overlap show data that goes into both sets.

Q1 A group of OAPs went to the beach for a day trip. The Venn diagram on the right shows how many wore a hat, sunglasses, both or neither.

a) How many OAPs went on the trip? ....

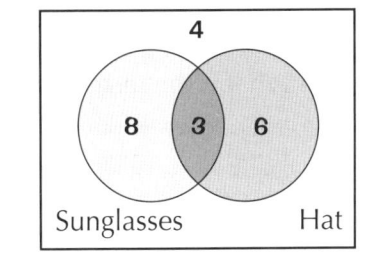

b) What's the probability that a randomly selected OAP is:

   i) wearing sunglasses? ....

   ii) wearing sunglasses and wearing a hat? ....

Q2 In a survey, **30** workers in an office were asked if they liked chocolate digestives, cookies or ginger biscuits. One person didn't like any of the biscuits (weirdo). Some of the results are shown in this Venn diagram.

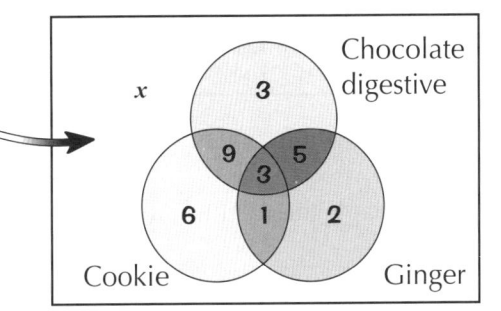

a) What is the value of x in the diagram?

   ....

b) What is the probability that a worker, chosen at random, likes ginger biscuits?

   ....

c) What is the probability that a worker, chosen at random, likes cookies and chocolate digestives, but not ginger biscuits?

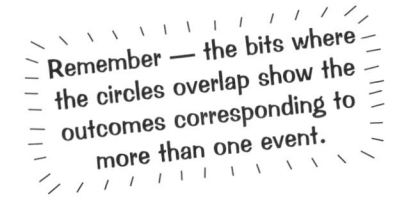

   ....

Remember — the bits where the circles overlap show the outcomes corresponding to more than one event.

Q3 A group of children on an outdoor pursuits course are given a choice of events to try. The results of who wants to do what are shown in the Venn diagram below:

a) How many are in the group?

   ....

b) How many want to do canoeing?

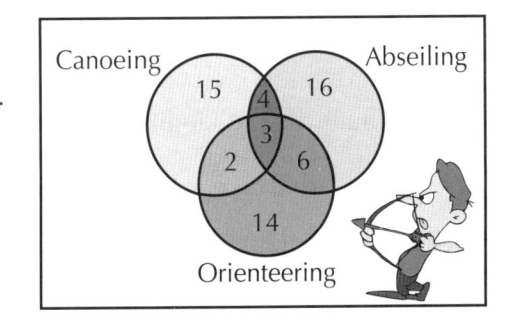

   ....

c) If you picked a child from the group at random:

   i) What is the probability of him or her wanting to do all three activities? ....

   ii) What is the probability of the child only wanting to do orienteering? ....

SECTION FOUR — PROBABILITY

Relative Frequency

Relative frequency is all about using trials to estimate the probability of something happening next. E.g. if I've had to make eight out of the last ten cups of tea for the office, will I have to make the next one? Grumble grumble grumble...

Q1 Neil flips a coin 15 times. It lands on heads eight times.

What is the relative frequency of getting a head after these 15 flips?

....

Q2 A shop sells green and red umbrellas. The owner is trying to work out the probability that the next brolly he sells will be green, not red. He records the number of green brollies and the number of red brollies he sells in a week.

red	red	green	red	green	red
green	green	green	green	red	red
green	red	red	green	red	green

Derek decided that it doesn't matter what colour brolly you have in a thunderstorm.

a) What is the total number of brollies sold? ....

b) What is the total number of green brollies sold? ....

c) Estimate the probability of him selling a green brolly next. ....

Q3 Simon spins a spinner 50 times. He records the number of times it lands on '1' in the first 10, 20 and 50 spins in the table below.

Number of spins	10	20	50
Number of 1s spun	3	6	13
Relative frequency			

a) Complete the table above.

b) From this table what is the best estimate of the probability of spinning a '1'?

....

Q4 a) What's the probability of rolling a 4 on a standard six-sided dice? ....

A six-sided dice is thrown 100 times and 45 fours are recorded.

b) i) Calculate the relative frequency of rolling a 4.

....

Remember — biased means some numbers are more likely to come up than others.

ii) Do you think the dice is biased? ....

iii) Give a reason for your answer. ....

SECTION FOUR — PROBABILITY

Expected and Actual Frequencies

You can predict the expected frequency of an outcome in a certain number of trials if you know the probability of that outcome occurring. But the actual frequency you get if you do the trials might be slightly different. Exciting stuff.

Expected frequency = number of trials × probability

Q1 A standard dice is thrown 60 times.

    a) i) What is the probability of throwing a 2? ....

    ii) What is the expected frequency of the number 2 being thrown? ....

    b) i) What is the probability of throwing a number less than 4? ....

    ii) What is the expected frequency of a number less than 4 being thrown? ....

Q2 A factory produces chocolate penguins and boxes of chocolate frogs.

There is a 5% probability that the penguins are misshapen.
The factory produces 280 chocolate penguins in an hour.

I'm not sharing a box with that misshapen frog...

    a) What is the expected number of misshapen penguins produced per hour?

....

There is a 10% probability that any box of frogs will fail a quality check.
160 boxes of frogs are checked for quality each day.

    b) How many boxes would you expect to fail the quality check each day?

....

Q3 A crisp manufacturer claims that one in every five packets of crisps has an instant-win prize in it.

    a) Out of sixty packets of crisps, how many packets would you expect to contain a prize?

....

Archie decides to test the claim and buys five packets of crisps.

    b) How many times do you expect Archie to win?

....

He doesn't win in any of them and concludes the manufacturer's claim must be false.

    c) i) Is Archie's conclusion correct? ....

    ii) Explain your answer.

....

....

SECTION FOUR — PROBABILITY

Probability Laws One

The first thing to think about when tackling one of these questions is whether the events can happen at the same time — if they can't they're called mutually exclusive.

Q1 Say whether the following pairs of events are **mutually exclusive** or **not**.

a) When picking a card at random from a standard pack of cards:
'getting a heart' and 'getting an ace'.

....

b) 'Winning the National Lotto' and 'not winning the National Lotto' with the same set of numbers in the same draw.

....

c) When selecting a person at random from a group of joggers:
'getting a man with black trainers' and 'getting a man with white shorts'.

....

d) When throwing a dice: 'getting a 6' and 'getting a 4'.

....

This picture has nothing to do with these questions, but it made me chuckle.

Q2 Daphne has a box of crisps that contains:
3 packets of cheese and onion
5 packets of roast chicken
4 packets of salt and vinegar

a) How many packets of crisps does the box contain altogether? ....

Daphne selects a packet from the box at random. Find the probability that she gets:

b) cheese and onion

....

c) roast chicken

....

d) salt and vinegar

....

e) cheese and onion **or** salt & vinegar

....

f) roast chicken **or** salt & vinegar

....

Don't forget, if the question says **OR** you **add** the probabilities together.

SECTION FOUR — PROBABILITY

Probability Laws One

Q3 George uses the spinner on the right to decide which kind of film to see.
Each section represents a different type of film.
There are three mutually exclusive categories:

A = action
C = comedy
S = science fiction

Find the probability that the film he selects is:

a) a comedy

....

b) comedy **or** action

....

c) comedy **or** action **or** science fiction

....

Q4 Carolyn picks a card at random from a standard pack of 52 cards.

a) What is the probability of Carolyn getting a club?

....

b) What is the probability of Carolyn getting a club **or** getting a heart **or** getting a spade?

....

c) What is the probability of Carolyn **not** getting a 5?
Hint: The probability of not getting an outcome = 1 – the probability of getting the outcome.

....

Q5 Alicia and Ben enter a raffle. There is a single prize, which will be awarded to the person who owns the selected ticket. Of the 50 tickets available, Alicia buys 30 and Ben buys 20.

a) Calculate the probabilities of each winning the raffle.

   Alicia: ....   Ben: ....

b) i) Are these events exhaustive? ....

   ii) Explain your answer.

   ....

   ....

SECTION FOUR — PROBABILITY

Probability Laws Two

There's always one rule for one and one rule for another, isn't there? Events which have no effect on each other are independent, which means you can multiply the probabilities to find out how likely they are to happen together.

Q1 Jack, Chloe and Sophie each want to order a takeaway for their dinner. The probability of each of them ordering pizza is:
Jack = 0.4.
Chloe = 0.7.
Sophie = 0.1.

If these probabilities are independent find the probability that:

a) Jack **and** Chloe will order pizza.

....

b) Chloe **and** Sophie will order pizza.

....

c) Jack **and** Chloe **and** Sophie will order pizza.

....

*Remember, if the question says **AND** you **multiply** the probabilities together.*

Q2 Gillian is designing a new school sweatshirt. She selects a colour by putting the names of **five colours** (green, red, blue, burgundy and black) in a bag and randomly selecting one.

She then tosses a coin to decide whether the sweatshirt should be **round-necked** or **V-necked**.

Calculate the probability of Gillian choosing:

a) a blue sweatshirt

....

b) a round-necked sweatshirt

....

c) a sweatshirt that is blue **and** has a round neck

....

d) a sweat shirt that is green **and** has a v-neck

....

SECTION FOUR — PROBABILITY

Probability Laws Two

Q3 'Malcolm's Car Sales' have a new car to be won.
All you need to do is throw a **6** with a standard dice **five times** in a row.

Calculate the probability of winning the car.

....

If several events are independent, just keep multiplying to find out the probability of them all happening.

Q4 If you pick one card from each of three separate packs of 52 cards, what's the probability that you will end up with three Kings?

....

Q5 Dave is baking cakes. The probability of him leaving a cake in the oven too long is always **0.15**.

If he bakes four cakes, what is the probability that he **forgets** about **at least one** of the cakes?

....

....

Don't forget — the probability of at least one event occurring is 1 – (the probability of none of them occurring).

Q6 The probability that Katie will go to France this summer is 0.6.
The probability that Daniel will go to France this summer is 0.3.

Assuming that these probabilities are independent, find the probability that:

a) both Katie **and** Daniel will go to France.

....

b) Katie won't go to France. ....

c) Daniel won't go to France. ....

d) neither Katie nor Daniel will go to France this summer.

....

SECTION FOUR — PROBABILITY

Tree Diagrams

Tree diagrams are really useful for working out probabilities. They're likely to come up in the exam, so make sure you can do them. Don't forget — you can easily check your diagrams by making sure that the end results add up to 1.

Q1 From the tree diagram shown:

a) Calculate the probability of passing both History and French.

....

....

b) Calculate the probability of failing French **and** passing History.

....

Q2 There are ten cars in a race. Seven are red and three are blue.
They all compete in two races. In both races, all the cars have an equal probability of winning.

a) Complete the tree diagram below to show the probability that the winner of each race is either red or blue.

First Race **Second Race**

.... Red winner
...... / Red winner <
               .... Blue winner

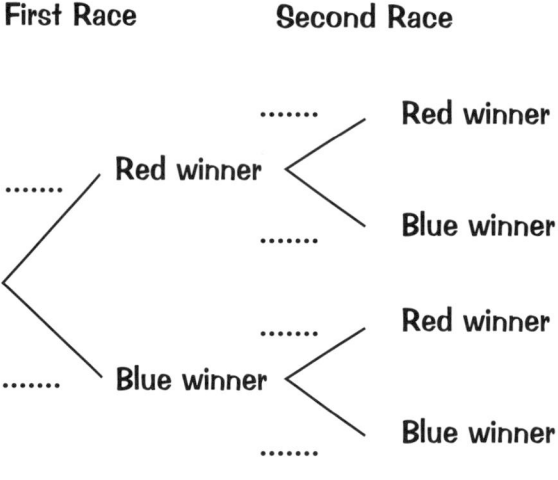

               .... Red winner
...... \\ Blue winner <
               .... Blue winner

b) Find the probability that the winner of both races is **red**.

....

c) Find the probability that the winner of the 1st race is **red** and the winner of the 2nd race is **blue**.

....

SECTION FOUR — PROBABILITY

Tree Diagrams

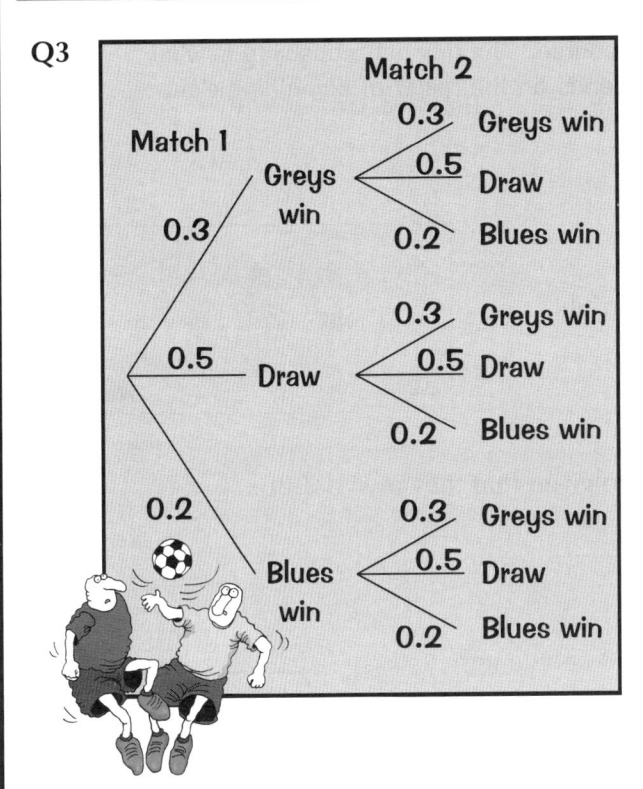

Q3

Match 1 / Match 2 tree diagram:
- Match 1: Greys win (0.3), Draw (0.5), Blues win (0.2)
- Match 2 (from Greys win): Greys win 0.3, Draw 0.5, Blues win 0.2
- Match 2 (from Draw): Greys win 0.3, Draw 0.5, Blues win 0.2
- Match 2 (from Blues win): Greys win 0.3, Draw 0.5, Blues win 0.2

The Greys and the Blues play two football matches. The tree diagram on the left shows the probabilities of different outcomes (Greys win, Blues win, or the match is a draw) for each of the matches.

a) Calculate the probability that the **Blues** will win **both** the matches.

....

b) Calculate the probability that the **Greys** will win **both** the matches?

....

c) What is the probability that the same team will win **both** of the matches?
Hint: it could be either the Blues OR the Greys.

....

Q4 There are two episodes of Gemma's favourite soap on Sunday. The probability of Gemma watching either episode is 0.4.

a) Complete this tree diagram:

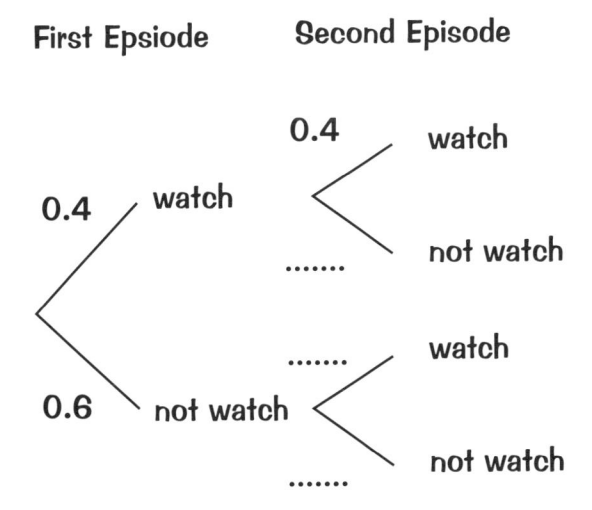

First Episode → Second Episode

- watch (0.4) → watch (0.4), not watch (.......)
- not watch (0.6) → watch (.......), not watch (.......)

b) Find the probability of her watching **both** episodes.

....

c) Find the probability of her **watching** the first episode and **not watching** the second.

....

d) Find the probability of her watching **only one** episode.
Hint: only one episode means watching only the first OR only the second episode.

....

SECTION FOUR — PROBABILITY

Conditional Probability

This page is just for people doing the AQA course. Conditional probability is when the probability of something happening depends on the result of something else.

Q1 100 people were asked if they own either a Z-Box or a Woo games console. The results are shown in the Venn diagram on the right.

Venn diagram: 40 outside; Z-Box only 18; intersection 8; Woo only 34.

a) How many people own a Z-Box?

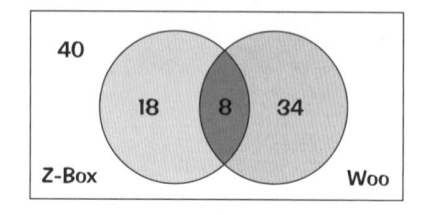

....

b) What is the probability of someone owning a Woo **given that** they own a Z-Box.

....

Q2 This table shows the results of a survey asking 150 people if they prefer hip-hop or pop music:

	Hip-Hop	Pop	Total
Male	32	33	65
Female	48	37	85
Total	80	70	150

What is the probability that a randomly chosen person from the survey:

a) is male **given that** they prefer pop music. ....

b) likes hip-hop **given that** they are female. ....

Q3 A survey was carried out to find out what types of sport people watch on the TV. The Venn diagram shows the results.

Venn diagram (Athletics, Football, Cricket): outside 4; Athletics only 9; Football only 28; Cricket only 13; Athletics ∩ Football only 12; Athletics ∩ Cricket only 18; Football ∩ Cricket only 11; all three 5.

a) What's the probability of someone watching cricket **given that** they watch football.

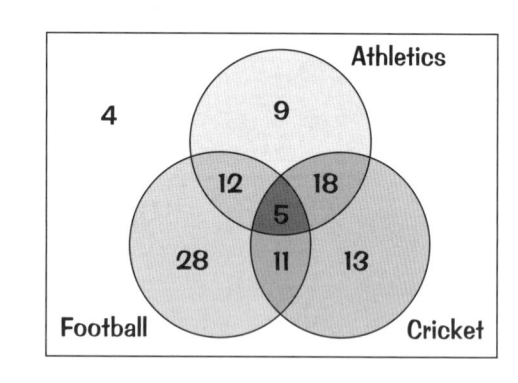

....
....

b) i) How many people in total said they watched athletics?

....

ii) What's the probability of someone watching football **and** cricket **given that** they watch athletics.

....

Mixed Questions

You need to be able to deal with probability questions that test you on lots of different things all mixed up together. So have a bash at these and you'll be sorted.

Q1 Cathy throws a ball repeatedly to Rob. Rob has to try and catch it with alternate hands. Cathy throws the ball **90** times to each of Rob's hands and records whether he catches or drops it. The results are shown in the table below.

	Left hand	Right hand	Total
Caught		76	
Dropped	64		
Total		90	

a) Complete the two-way table.

b) Using the results of all 180 throws, calculate the **relative** frequency of Rob:

i) catching the ball. ....

ii) dropping the ball. ....

c) Cathy and Rob decide to play the same game again. What is the **expected** frequency of catches made if the total number of throws is 70?

....

Q2 Alex draws a card from a standard 52-card deck.

a) i) What is the probability of him drawing a heart?

....

ii) What is the probability of him drawing a heart **or** a diamond?

....

b) What is the probability of him drawing an ace **or** a king?

....

Alex draws a card from the deck and replaces it. Then he draws a second card from the deck.

c) What is the probability of him drawing two black cards?
Hint: Replacing the card means the two events are independent.

....

d) What is the probability of him drawing two aces?

....

SECTION FOUR — PROBABILITY

Mixed Questions

Q3 In a typical one-month period 98% of all trains arriving in a station are on time. The probability of a train arriving on time does not depend on what happens to any other train.

a) i) What is the probability of a train being late? ....

ii) What is the expected frequency of late trains next month, when 350 trains will run?

....

b) i) Calculate the probability that **no trains** are **late** out of **four** arriving in the station. Give your answer to 4 significant figures.

....

ii) Calculate the probability that **at least one** train is **late** out of **four** arriving in the station.

....

Q4 People living in a village were asked what kind of material they regularly recycled. The results are shown in the Venn diagram below.

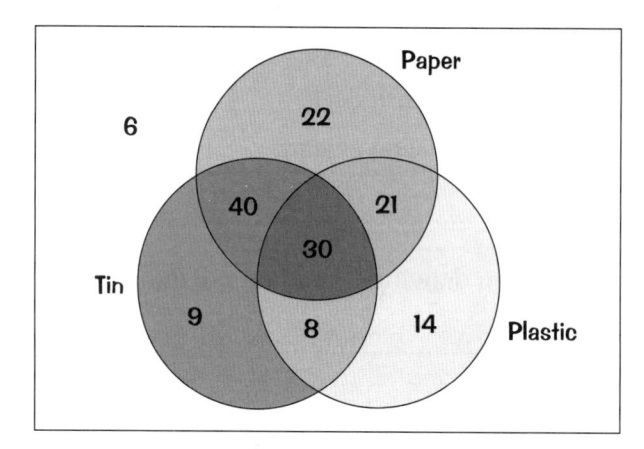

[Venn diagram with three circles labelled Tin, Paper, Plastic. Values: 6 (outside), Paper only 22, Tin only 9, Plastic only 14, Tin∩Paper only 40, Paper∩Plastic only 21, Tin∩Plastic only 8, Tin∩Paper∩Plastic 30]

a) How many people were included in the survey? ....

b) A person is selected at random. What is the probability that they:

i) recycle paper? ....

ii) only recycle one type of material? ....

iii) recycle tin given that they recycle paper and plastic? ....

SECTION FOUR — PROBABILITY